Finding Freedom

Angela C. Rowe

Scripture quotations are taken from the NIV version of the *Holy Bible*.

Cover Design by Laura E. Schlatter

Printed in the United States of America

GIG Publishing, Benton, AR. 72015

www.gigpublishing.com

ISBN: 978-0-578-80859-8

Dedication

For, Rehema, who loved her grandchild endlessly and trusted that God would bring someone to save him. Without you, we would have never known one of the greatest blessings of our lives.

"But those who hope in the LORD will renew their strength. They will soar on wings like eagles; they will run and not grow weary, they will walk and not be faint."

-Isaiah 40:31

"LORD, you are my God; I will exalt you and praise your name, for in perfect faithfulness you have done wonderful things, things planned long ago."

-Isaiah 25:1

Thank You

*Thank you to my amazing husband, Brian. Without your constant love, support, and encouragement, I would have never had the strength to see this project to completion. You are my heart and soul. I have loved you since I could remember, and I would never trade our crazy, adventurous life for anything normal.

*Thank you to my beautiful girls, Emily and Bekah. Your 45 minutes of begging to bring home a baby, "just for the night," changed all of our lives forever. I can never thank you enough for not stopping until I said yes.

*Thank you to my wonderful boys, Andrew and Morgan. You stepped in and became an instant big brother to our surprise baby. You have loved and cared deeply for a brother you never knew you needed. And that love has changed the direction of his precious life.

*Thank you, Joseph Freedom, for being our precious, baby boy. Being your mom is one of the biggest blessings of my life. I can't wait to see the plan and purpose God has for you. You are a life changer!

*Thank you, GIG Publishing, for taking this project on. I'm so grateful God brought you into our lives to allow you to be a part of His amazing story. We are so blessed to have you in our lives.

Table of Contents

"I will not leave you as orphans; I will come to you."

-John 14:18

Introduction

Just the beginning...

When the local police finally arrived, they found a small house with a dry and dusty front yard. From the outside, it looked normal, except, for the little, crumpled body of a baby boy, sprawled on the ground. He became a regular sight to all the passing neighbors, until they could no longer handle his agonizing muffled cries for help. The police stood over his body staring at what they thought was the body of a dead, emaciated infant. To their surprise, the little body moved just slightly. It was enough for them to recognize that this little one still had just enough life left, to let them know he was still alive.

The police stood in absolute shock. It went from a body recovery to a rescue mission. They very gently picked up his frail, broken body, and quickly whisked him off to the local hospital. They then turned their attention to the woman who lived there. The stepmother of this baby boy was arrested for attempted murder. She would be released, to her husband, just a few hours later, but not before the hospital report was given to the arresting officer.

The hospital found that this infant was actually closer to two years old. This would not have been obvious to the naked eye being that he weighed in at slightly above ten pounds, with severe malnutrition, due to starvation. That alone was startling, but the injuries kept coming. This baby boy had suffered from skin melting burns, across his chest, from hot cereal that had been poured over him. He had a black eye and various random bruising from head to toe. And his hip was either broken, or completely displaced, from being kicked off a front porch. The hospital could find no reason why his little body had not given out before now. To this day, the police still refer to this little boy as the most severe child abuse case in this city's history.

He was not expected to live...

⁴ On the day you were born your cord was not cut, nor were you washed with water to make you clean, nor were you rubbed with salt or wrapped in cloths. ⁵ No one looked on you with pity or had compassion enough to do any of these things for you. Rather, you were thrown out into the open field, for on the day you were born you were despised.

⁶ "'Then I passed by and saw you kicking about in your blood, and as you lay there in your blood I said to you, "Live!"

-Ezekiel 16:4-6

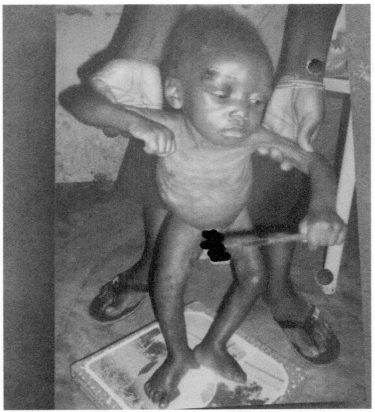

Joseph at police station after they found him. He was two years old. The police were documenting his state of wellbeing. They had him hold a pen for size comparison of his actual body. (Certain parts of the picture have been blacked out).

Chapter 1

Compass Rowes

"And He said to them "Go into the world and preach the gospel to all creation."

-Mark 16:15

We left for Uganda wondering what our new life would hold. We had more questions than we had answers, but we had more faith than we had doubt. That was enough for us. Being foreign missionaries was something we wanted to do for more than twelve years. People asked us why we weren't on the mission field by that time. I wanted to reply, "We have no idea, but if God gives you the answer, please let us know!" But instead, I gave them the typical, church answer. "The Lord has not opened the door for us to leave yet."

It wasn't because we weren't knocking. We were knocking on the door like a two-year-old who was potty training. Brian must have contacted fifty organizations in the beginning. We even had to buy ourselves an official looking laptop bag to hold all the information coming in from all the different organizations. If there's one thing to know about me, I love shopping for office supplies and cleaning supplies, but that's neither here nor there. What we didn't know then, was He was waiting for the perfect time and for something so big it would change not only our lives, but the lives of an entire village.

Brian and I, getting off the plane, with our three children, Andrew (18), Emily (14), Morgan (12), and Bekah (18) (who would one day be my daughter-in-love), in a new country, in the dead of night, was not the typical, welcoming experience I thought it would be. Neither did it give me the warm fuzzies I pictured as we started our new life. In fact, the more we drove further into Uganda, and away from the airport, my stress level got higher and higher. I have a huge sense of adventure, but it came with an even bigger sense of fear. Anyone can be an armchair quarterback, but it's not until your feet hit the field that you know what you are made of.

As we made our way into Kampala, the capital city, the air was thick and choking with smoke from the little campfires dotted along the side of the road. I remember uttering these words for the first time, "Lord, what have we done?" I also looked at Brian before we left sunny, Southern California and said, "I don't want to go camping for the rest of my life." By the way things looked and smelled I was sure I would be earning numerous scouting badges before I left this country. Man, I had no idea how true that would be! I definitely earned the "crying-every-day-for-a-year" badge. Is that a badge? Well, who do I call? And yes, that was a true survival skill.

Settling into missionary life was not glamorous. Some days we had electricity and on others we were in the dark. We always seemed to have water, although, it always had to be filtered. We had hot showers, only if we had power. And that hot shower only filtered through, what we were introduced to as, the "electric shower

7

head." Now, I did listen in science class. I know that's surprising, but my take away from that was – not to mix water and electricity. Here I was, telling my kids to go take a shower with the very thing I knew could electrocute them. It was a gamble and actually worked...until it didn't. That's when you thought you were showering with a life sized clown, who was joyfully pushing a buzzer, causing you to be zapped from time to time. My phrase for the next two years was, "We are going to laugh about this someday." I was going to have to dig deep if I was going to survive in my new world.

We tell people, anyone can handle a short-term mission trip. You enter the country of your choice and stay for a short period of time, and in your hand is a return ticket. You don't have to juggle what it takes to start a new life in a culture you don't understand. It was that little fact that brought me to my knees. No return flights! I knew God had gotten us in, and only He was going to get us out. No matter how hard days were going to be, I had to trust this was His plan for our lives. I knew God was good. I also knew that I would eventually find joy in this journey. And I would eventually stop allowing fear to be my tour guide by embracing the dreams God had dreamed for us. This was the calling I had felt since I was fourteen years old. I looked around at my less than inviting surroundings and thought, "Why didn't I just become a flight attendant?"

We had been in Uganda for a month, when out of nowhere, a little bundle (and I mean little bundle) was dropped into our laps. His name was Joseph, and we were told he was two years old. I didn't believe a word of it. There was no possible way he could be. He was the size of a twelve-month-old, if that. One Sunday, at the international church we attended, Emily walked up to Brian and me and said, "Wanna hold him?" I will never forget the first time I held that boy in my arms. At that time, I had no idea why it pierced my soul. I now know God wanted me to never forget the first time I held my son. I remember the first time I held all my children and this one would be no different.

He was tiny and had no expression. He sat so still. If it hadn't been for the chest cold and rattle in his lungs, I would have thought he wasn't breathing. He looked at Brian and me, with a blank stare, and it broke my heart. I wondered what this child had seen and endured in his little life. I remember telling Brian this baby was sick, but I also remember thinking in my little American mind, he would go back to the baby home for meds where, next week, he would be all better. That's how it worked for my kids. Never sick longer than a week or so. This was Africa, and I was about to find out Africa doesn't run on Western time.

This is the house Joseph was born in. The house is no longer there because the roof, which was made from cement, caved in. It belonged to Joseph's grandmother, Rehema.

Chapter 2

Gas Station Diapers

"The Spirit of God has made me; and the breath of the Almighty gives me life."

-Job 33:4

Sunday was finally here, and I walked into church with excitement, wanting to see him, but not wanting everyone else to know I felt that way. I could see all the babies from the baby home/orphanage lined up against the wall, sitting in chairs so sweetly. We took our seats and waited for the service to start. I could always count on Emily to run to the back and grab a baby. And sure enough, this day was no different (so I thought). Before I knew it, she was standing in front of me with a little sweet angel in her arms. What she said next would be forever burned into my mind. "Mom, look. Here's our baby from last week." OUR BABY. Yes, the baby I thought about all week. The baby I was surprisingly anticipating seeing today. I scooped him in my arms and held him the entire service. Poor Emily had to run to the back and pick another baby to hold because she was not getting this one back.

As I held him against my chest, the first thing I remember was the shocking feeling of the chest cold from the prior week, but this time it was far worse. I looked at Brian and said, with shock and sadness, "He's still sick." He lay against my chest with no movement except, for his tiny finger playing with my earring, lightly batting it back and forth. With every breath he took, I could feel it was more of a struggle than the last time I held him. At some point, this sweet baby got emotional, but I would have never known had Brian not looked over at us. Brian whispered, "He's crying." I thought, "There's no way!" He has not moved or even made a sound of any kind. I pulled him up from my chest and saw big tears coming down his face. It absolutely broke my heart. I wiped his face and said to Brian, "Do you want to hold him?" He carefully took this little one in his arms and laid him on his chest. I remember not being able to look away. It was the sweetest and

13

saddest moment. Brian was a father to this sweet little angel if only for the length of a church service. And this little one was cradled, loved, and soothed by a family who instantly fell in love with him.

I spent the following week thinking about this baby I had held during our church service. It didn't matter what I was doing around the house. Out of nowhere, thoughts of this baby came flooding in. I wondered how he was, what he was doing, and if he was any better. As the next Sunday approached, I started to get excited and hopeful to get to see this little one I held the week before. I was still baffled by my emotions towards him. We worked with kids every day. Why a pull towards this one?

After the service, we found ourselves standing at the front of the church, holding this baby, and talking to the "owner" of the baby home/orphanage. He was a very charismatic, Danish man, who had been in Uganda, for the past ten years and loved what he did there. He saw us holding Joseph and asked if we wanted to take him for the night. In a nano-second, I had a million hesitations, with as many questions to match. I instantly said, "Noooo!" This was a baby, not a puppy. I didn't want to borrow a baby! I was sure this baby had enough abandonment issues without us adding to them. The thought of that nearly broke my heart.

Our charismatic, Danish friend let me know his heart was to have every child in his baby home feel the love of a family at some point in their life. For the next forty-five minutes, Emily and Bekah worked Brian and I over. Begging and pleading with us to let us take him home. I said, "He's not a puppy. We can't do this to him." Even the manager, who was waiting for Joseph to be put in the van, so he could return him to the orphanage, was hesitant. But, because of the voice of the very charismatic baby homeowner saying, "Yes, do this! Love on him for the night," I very reluctantly found myself saying, "Ok. Just for the night, but you girls are helping!" We loaded our family in a tiny pickup truck and started the engine. My next breath was, "DIAPERS! We need diapers!!!" Where do you get diapers in our little trading village, in the heart of Uganda? I yelled out the window to the manager that very question. Her response was, "At the petrol station. The one at the corner." Right, this was not America! Buying gas station diapers should not have surprised me, but it did! If I had to buy diapers from a gas station, it better come with a blue raspberry Icee, a hot dog, and a vanilla scented pine tree for the rear-view mirror! Well, at least the diapers were bought that day.

We made it home from the gas station with our baby supplies and all our family, plus one, piled out of our truck, into our house. I remember feeling kind of awkward. I have this baby, out of nowhere, and I'm totally unprepared. He didn't come with a diaper bag or extra clothes. We didn't have toys he could play with or...FOOD! What about food? What do I feed him? We sat him on the couch and he instantly looked overwhelmed. All these new faces ooing and awing over him in a new place. It must have felt strange or even scary for this sweet little angel.

It was lunch time, and I knew I had to get the family fed. My thoughts were of this wee one, and what he could handle. I remember thinking years back, if I had to do it over again, I would make my own baby food, to ensure they were getting the best nutrients. Why? Why did I think this? Did the baby food industry really make it look that simple to me? Here was my chance. I went to the kitchen to see what instant organic baby food I could make. What I ended up making was a small bowl of mashed avocados. I brought it to him as though I had just made him the greatest meal he was ever going to get. I was beyond proud of myself, but the fight was on! It wasn't the food I presented to him. It was the spoon! He was accustomed to using his hands, and a utensil was as foreign as we were. The love for the avocado outweighed his dislike for the spoon, and in the end, he ended up eating the whole thing. Avocado and smashed pumpkin became his go-to foods, along with anything else I would let him put in his mouth.

With the tune, "Eye of the Tiger," playing in my head, I knew I had conquered lunch. Now, on to toys. He was so little I kept thinking he was around twelve months old, but that was not the case. I went to the kitchen once again to see if I could make him something that would hold his attention. I found an empty, garlic powder bottle, filled it with popcorn seeds, and ran into the living room to give to him. I very proudly presented the "toy." I made a rattle!!! I thought the little shaker was adorable, and he would just love the noise of it. He graciously received it, shook it a few times, and sat there. It wasn't until Morgan came into the room with some toy cars, did this little boy come to life. He grabbed the cars and knew exactly how to play with them. We all stood there in shock. We could not believe it. He had slid off the couch and turned around facing the couch, using the cushions as a table. He began pushing the cars and making car sounds. Being a little boy was universal. We understood two things in that moment, the joy that had filled his face and the car sound effects he was making as he played.

No matter how happy he was, it didn't erase the fact, he was still sick. In fact, as the day went on, he began to feel worse. Brian and I had a dinner arrangement that night we had to attend. We also had a college student from Utah staying with us, for a week, named Katie. Andrew, Bekah, and Katie were left in charge of the younger ones, which now included, Joseph. As we were getting in the car, I turned to see that Katie had strapped Joseph to her back, like a good Uganda momma would, as they would all be heading down the hill to the best burger place in town.

We had only been gone a few hours, and when we returned, we saw that baby Joseph had taken a turn for the worse. With every breath, his chest would sink so far in I thought I would see his spine. It was the most labored breathing I had ever witnessed. The other thing I noticed is he was naked, lying on a cold wet towel, on our concrete floor. Katie told me he was running a very, high fever and when she was little her mom did this for her and her siblings. She also said she thought he had pneumonia. When she was younger, she had pneumonia, and this is what it looked like.

I went and called the manager of the baby home right away, explaining the situation. I told her we suspected pneumonia, and she needed to send a nurse right away. I was told no one travels at night, and she would send someone first thing in the morning. My heart sank! Would he be alive in the morning? What would I do if I woke up to a dead baby in my house? How would I help my kids through this? We prayed for baby Joseph that night and asked God to heal his little body. The girls were very adamant about wanting him to sleep in their room so we put him in there for the night, and trusted God for the best.

The next morning, I opened the girl's door with great hesitation. I had no idea what I would find behind that door. Once the door was opened, what I found was a very sick baby. But he was alive, and the rest I could deal with. It wasn't long after we got him up there was a knock on the door. It was a little Ugandan lady who looked very weathered with time, but she was there to take charge of this sweet little one and get him to the hospital. We hugged and kissed him and sent him off, covered in love and much prayer.

Within a day or so, we received a phone call from the manager stating we were right about his condition. He had pneumonia and was going to die. I think I was shocked or stunned. I don't think I breathed for a few seconds. Die? He was just at my house. This was so mind numbing to me. I couldn't wrap my head around this. The next thing the manager said was "Will you come pray for him?" Fear flooded me. I answered with the first thing that came to mind, "No, I can't. I can't see a baby die." In my head I was screaming "I'm a sheltered American. The only dead people I ever saw were grandparents who were beautifully presented to us at a funeral home." The manager was very calm and said, "You are a local missionary, and when there is something like this, we call the missionaries to the hospital to pray." I think that's the first time I felt the weight of my calling. It hit me right between the eyes. I told her without hesitation I would come.

We arrived at the hospital right as the sun went down, which added to the eeriness of this place. It was like no hospital I had ever seen. We who live in the west, with western medicine, are so blessed. I had no idea just how blessed until I walked in and saw this place. I walked very quietly down two, dark, humid concrete hallways, until I reached a room lined with beds heaving with people. We were in the pediatric wing for sure. All the sick children in beds gave that away. Mothers and care takers sat next to the beds where their children lay. Baby Joseph was the second bed in the room. As we walked in, all faces turned towards us. A slight pause of surprised silence filled the room, and then, chatter exploded. We were white women, walking into this room. It was something you didn't see every day. I have no idea what was being said, but I can only imagine.

The size of the bed made little baby Joseph look that much smaller. He was in the cleanest hospital bed I had ever seen. The manager proceeded to tell me the caretaker had just washed the bed sheets, took them off the line, and remade the bed. I was surprised by that. I said, "What?" She then told me, in Uganda, you have to bring your own supplies to the hospital, such as linens and food. I had no idea! Baby Joseph was clean and content in the bed until he saw me. He turned his head away from me and refused to look at me. I picked him up, and I could instantly tell he was not happy to see me. The manager started laughing and said, "He's mad at you because the last time he saw you, he was at your house, and now he's here." We both had a good chuckle. I looked into that baby's face and began to pray. I prayed silently because I just wasn't sure how this was done, but I knew God would hear me. What I prayed next might have made me the worst missionary ever, but my heart was in the right spot. This was my prayer:

"Little man, the way I see it, you have two choices. I know what's outside this door, and to die would truly be gain. It's too harsh for little kids to make it here. So, if you want to go to Jesus, GO! I will find you once I get there, where you can show me around, and I will let you know all the crazy things I accomplished on earth. We can start our relationship in heaven. BUT...If you live, you live for God! That's it. Those are your choices."

I'm sure I ended it with "In Jesus' name I pray. Amen," because, that's how you end every great prayer. Yep, I was a stellar missionary! I knew at that point missions training should have been something we were made to do before we even left the states.

I laid baby Joseph down on his clean sheets where he rolled over and threw up all over them. I looked up in horror because I knew what the caretaker went through to get them that clean. I felt horrible. She very gently removed the sheets and sweetly said, "It's okay." And she truly meant it. The manager looked at me and said it was time to go. I took one last look at baby Joseph and knew the fight was his. I wasn't sure which way he would go, but I knew he was in the Lord's hands. I truly never expected to see him again, on this side of heaven, due to how sick he actually was, and how limited the treatments were.

We got on with the week, where our thoughts and prayers often floated back to our sweet baby Joseph. We wondered how he was. We hadn't received any news, so, we thought, no news was good news. Seven days later, our phone rang. It was the manager. I had braced myself for the news and what she said next took my breath away.

"You are not going to believe this. HE LIVED!"

"WHAT?" I replied.

"Yes, he lived and is leaving the hospital tomorrow. I have a question for you. Since you have respiratory therapy training, can he come stay at your house for a couple of months to rehabilitate?"

I had a million questions for her, but what I found coming out of my mouth, was a very excited YES!!!! Yes, he can come here. And training in respiratory therapy? My kids had colds and the flu and survived. That qualified me to take on this little one. Since he fought his way back from the brink of death, we were going to fight for his recovery... and for him (but I didn't know that until much later).

The front porch of the house we lived in while in Uganda.
In Uganda, they built houses backwards for privacy. So,
the front porch is facing the backyard.

The house up the driveway, straight ahead, is the back of our home, facing the front yard. The house to the right is our guesthouse.

Our guest house, to the right, of the main house.

Me, at our home in Uganda, holding an average sized avocado.

Emily giving Joseph his very 1st bath at our house. He was not too excited about that.

My son, Andrew, comforting baby Joseph after his first bath.

Chapter 3

Cloth Diapers are for Dusting, Right?

"This is what the Sovereign Lord says to these bones: I will make breath enter you, and you will come to life."

-Ezekiel 37:5 (NIV)

"WELCOME HOME", the dry erase board read as you walked into the house. The kids were so excited we were going to have a baby living in the house. We had no idea how this was going to work out, but we thought there were a lot of hands in the house and work would be light if we all worked together.

From the moment this little one came into our house, he had us wrapped around his tiny little finger. The manager walked in and saw our sign. She laughed and said, "Aw, you people need this boy." I think she was a little surprised we made such a big deal of him coming

31

since this was just going to be a short stay. We wanted him to know he was wanted and loved, even if he didn't fully understand, even if it was just temporary. The girls absolutely fussed over him. That sweet boy had three mommas in the house, a bag of medication, and a stack of cloth diapers. Wait...what? The manager handed me twelve cloth diapers and told me she may have more but, would have to look. CLOTH DIAPERS! Can I say it any louder? Where are my beautiful, disposable gas station diapers? She said this is what is provided by the baby home. You have got to be kidding me! I have never used a cloth diaper for anything but dusting. The last time I held a cloth diaper, it was covered in dust, not...

Since our funding was tight, disposable diapers didn't fit into our budget. This was for sure going to test me, and I wasn't so sure we would laugh about this one someday. I was wrong. We laugh so hard about our adventures with cloth diapers.

The phone rang very early the next morning. I stumbled to find my cell phone, and when I did finally answer, on the other end of the line was the very, charismatic, Danish, baby homeowner. He let me know he would be there in a matter of minutes, with a doctor, so baby Joseph could have his first follow-up appointment. I was still half asleep and not looking ready for company. I jumped into panic mode and got dressed. I grabbed the baby and readied him as fast as I could. Then it hit me. "House call!" I'm living in a place where the doctor makes house calls!!!! It was the greatest day of my life. At this point I had been a mother for eighteen years and hated loading up the car with all my kids to go across town and sit in a crowded waiting room. Visits took no less than two hours, most of the time, and usually, included me bribing them with stickers or suckers for good behavior. You are telling me in this country the doctor comes to your front door!!! I was beyond excited.

In ten minutes, there was a knock on the door, and in walked the very, charismatic, Danish owner, with a very, quiet and reserved young, Ugandan doctor. His name was John Bosco. Their friendship started when John Bosco was a child. The Danish owner told me this man had become his family doctor, and he trusted him wholeheartedly. He took baby Joseph into his arms, and the first thing he said to me was, "Thank you for caring for this boy." I was a little surprised by that. I came to realize it was a custom the Ugandan people did. They were very thankful to see the children of their country being cared for, especially, by people who didn't have to.

It didn't take him long to give us his evaluation of Joseph. He said his lungs would clear up, as long as we kept giving him his medication. He also said he was still suffering from malnutrition (even though, he had been in protective custody for four months). He let us know baby Joseph's facial muscles were so deteriorated, he would not show any emotion for about six months. So, we weren't supposed to push him to smile. That's when I flashed back to the church service, I held him in, where he was crying with no facial expression. It all made sense to me now. The doctor assured us, besides all of that, he was expecting the boy to make a full recovery.

Over the next two weeks, we settled into our new routine with baby Joseph. He came into our lives not knowing how to speak or walk. These were the things we were going to be working on. The muscles in his whole body were so eaten away from malnutrition. He had very, little leg control. I remember working with him to get him to stand up by the coffee table. We had taken him to see a British physical therapist, who spent some time with him, watching him move. He scooted on his bottom to get anywhere. She let us know that he was in good, physical condition, all things considered, and it would be a matter of time to build the hip muscles back up. She also said the reason he cried when forced to do the leg exercises was not from pain, but rather, it felt weird to him to where he didn't like it.

We were going to need to help push him through it if he was ever going to be able to walk. Joseph would not only walk one day, but he would say his superpower is kicking a soccer ball. He started making little milestones. It was during those first two weeks, he started talking. With all the American mouths in the house, there was no way he was going to stay silent for long.

His first words in Luganda were, "give me" and "mine". A local friend stopped by our house one night and heard him talking. He asked us if we knew what he was saying, to which we told him, we had no idea. That's when he told us what he was saying in Luganda. He was not only speaking Luganda, but he was speaking words we understood. JoJo (the nickname I gave him) started speaking. He was speaking English! We were communicating with this sweet little angel. His first words, "Mommy" and "Daddy"! That's what he called us because that's what he heard our kids calling us. It didn't bother us in the least. He was ours until the Lord saw different.

One of JoJo's favorite things to do was to go outside with Brian. We had found a toddler swing in the garage, left by the previous people, and Brian hung it in a tree for Joseph. One afternoon, Brian took Joseph outside, and put him in the swing. Moments later, as I'm standing in the kitchen, I hear Brian yelling for me to come as fast as

I can. My heart sank. I had no idea what had happened or what I would see when I looked. I ran to the window as fast as I could, and what I saw took my breath away. Brian was pushing Joseph in the swing and he was laughing. REALLY laughing! There it was, two weeks in, and his facial muscles and emotions woke up. We finally got to hear his laugh and the joy that spilled out of his first moments of "firsts". Who knew his first swing, would awaken his first laugh, but God? It wasn't six months, like the doctor predicted. It was two weeks. I contacted the doctor right away and told him what had taken place. He told me that only the power of love could have woken up those frozen muscles and again, thanked us for caring for this boy.

The "Welcome Home" sign my daughter, Emily, made for Joseph.

Joseph's stuffed animals hanging out to dry. He slept with them every night. He was sick and threw up on them, therefore, they had to be washed.

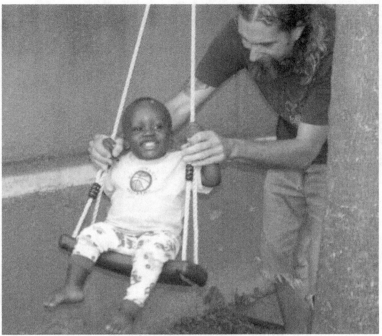

"Joseph's First Smile"

Top, left to right: My daughter, Emily, my son, Morgan, and my daughter in law, Bekah. Bottom, left to right: Angela, Joseph, Brian, and my son, Andrew.

Left to right: My daughter, Emily, and my daughter in law, Bekah, kissing JoJo.

My son, Andrew, and my daughter in law, Bekah.

Chapter 4

Life in Katwe

He says, "Be still and know I am God; I will be exalted among the nations, I will be exalted in the earth."

-Psalm 46:10 (NIV)

Do you know most cities in Uganda have a "Katwe"? We pronounce it, Cat-Way. We thought it was just a suburb of Masaka, the little trading center/town we were living in. We began to notice, when we went to Kampala, for our monthly grocery store run, the locals there would ask us where we stayed in Masaka. We would tell them, Katwe. At this point, there would be a million different expressions flashed across their faces. But, in the end, they would say, "You need to stay somewhere different. We can't believe you are making it there." We would always tell them that Katwe is beautiful and our compound is breathtaking. We lived in a large house, with two guest houses, on the same property. It sits on a hill where the breeze makes the heat bearable. The grounds are covered in beautiful tropical plants, and we even had tropical fruit trees in the front and back yards. It was really the most beautiful place we have had the opportunity to live. It wasn't until we got home, to America, we found out that Katwe means "SLUMS."

The baby home gave us a crib for JoJo. We put him in the corner of the living room. That little piece of the house became his spot every night. We would put him in his crib and cover it with a mosquito net, followed by a white bed sheet, so he would fall asleep with all of us still in the room. We laughed because we felt like we were putting a bird to bed every night.

On some occasions, he was still awake, when we turned out the lights. We would hear a sweet little voice, coming from inside the little, covered, baby fort saying, "Ha-yo, daddy ha-yo." We chuckled, and we assured him he wasn't alone. Our room was right off the living room, just on the other side of the wall. When morning came, if we happened to still be asleep, when his sweet little eyes opened up, we would awake to the same greeting. "Ha-yo daddy, ha-yo?" ("Ha-yo" meant "hello).

Two months after Joseph had come to stay with us, it just began to feel natural to have him in our lives, daily. He just felt seamless, as if he had always been here. We found ourselves at one of the many Danish parties one night, when our charismatic, Danish friend asked us if we wanted to adopt Joseph. He said it so nonchalantly, as if asking us if we wanted a piece of cake. His tone was so sweet and encouraging, when the question came out, we found ourselves saying, "Yes." We looked at each other with that questioning look in our eye, as if to say, "We do?" We did, but we knew we had no means in which to do that.

It was at that point, the baby home manager spoke up, with a very shocked tone and said, "Wait! No, they can't adopt him. Joseph is not adoptable. He has living relatives." A sigh of relief yet, sadness, hit me at the same time. We learned later, children in Uganda, who have living relatives, cannot be adopted and to do so was illegal. That's the terminology that was used when the manager told us. We left the party that night feeling like a bag of mixed emotions.

The project we had been sent to Uganda to do, plus, caring for a baby, all in the first few months of being in a new country, were starting to take its toll on us. Our Danish friends saw this and told us we needed to get away for a week or so and regroup. He said all missionaries need to do this. It's absolutely necessary for the longevity of your mission to step back and take a breather. He and his wife offered their home they had in another city called Jinja.

We had heard nothing but amazing things about this place. It's the "birthplace" of the Nile River. The river ran through the town and people from all over the world went there to float its amazing rapids. The NILE! The place we had read about in the Bible since we were little kids in Sunday school. We had to go! We could not wait to see it in person. I love history and to put my feet in the very waters that God used to set the freedom of the Israelites into motion was beyond amazing to me. It made me speechless.

I could go on for pages about the majesty of the Nile. It did not disappoint at all. The moment I saw it, I could have just wept. Who were we to get this moment in time? God had blessed the Rowe family. As we stood there with mouths wide open, we took in the beauty that this amazing place offered up to us. As I reflect on the moment, as we all stood on the riverbank, I'm really beginning to think that it was more than just a two-week vacation. I think it might have been symbolic for the journey we were about to embark upon. God used the Nile to set freedom in motion for His people, and I think it was no different for us as well. Freedom was going to be our mission and fighting for it was going to be our calling.

We loved the peace and family time we were having in Jinja. This sweet little town was everything that people had ever said it was. We had the chance to meet other missionaries that actually got to live there and see what they were doing. There was nothing sweeter than being surrounded by like-minded people, who were sent to the same continent as we were. The like-mindedness made us feel not so alone. God kept doing that for us along the way. That breath to keep going became our lifeline.

As we were enjoying our time, the phone rang and it was the manager of the baby home. She said Joseph's mother had turned up at the baby home looking for him because she had heard from someone in town, he was dying. She had also heard that Joseph was living with "white people" and wanted to see if we were caring for him properly. All of that surprised us since she abandoned him a year before this. Why the sudden compassion? We were told she was only curious about the "white people" rumor. The manager told her that indeed he was staying with us and it had improved the quality of his life. It was at that time the manager told us the mother wanted to set up a meeting so she could see him and us for herself. I started to panic! What if this was the beginning of the end for us? What if?...What if?...What if?

I can tell you, God does not dwell in the land of what ifs. He can be trusted, and peace in this shaky moment was mine if I took the gift He was offering. I was assured this wasn't a "give back". It was just a "checkup". I was not going to forfeit my peace and go through the rest of our trip upset so, I had to hand this over to the Lord. If God wanted this baby with us, he would stay. I only had to BE STILL.

It would take another six months for that face to face meeting. In those six months, God and I had some major talks and so did Brian and I. We knew God wanted Joseph to stay with us for the time being, and we knew he felt like our son. But what we didn't know is if it was just temporary or if it was going to be made permanent. On two occasions, I was standing in the kitchen cooking and cleaning when I began to speak to God about Joseph. I said to God, "God, can we really have a child from a baby home style living, staying in a western lifestyle type home, only to give him back? I feel like that will give him more issues than he walked in here with."

Joseph had already been abandoned once in his little life. I didn't want to make it twice, and this time, he was older and would remember it. It was at that point, I heard the Lord say, "If I came back today, I would find you doing exactly what I want you doing." That was it for me. I knew regardless of the outcome, Joseph had to be with us. For how long, was up to the Lord. The second time God spoke to me, I froze in my tracks. Joseph had this stealthy way about him. He could scoot around on his bottom so fast and not make a sound. Every night, when I was cooking dinner, he would make his way into the kitchen and sit at my feet as I cooked. I use to think he just wanted to be next to me, but I now think he wanted to sample whatever I was cooking before it actually ended up on the table. He learned fast that the kitchen was where all the magic happened in our house.

Well, on this night, it was no different, so I thought. He had silently made his way in the kitchen, and I had no idea. When I quickly turned around and found him sitting in the middle of our big kitchen floor, it startled me a bit, but what I heard next, I hope I never forget. I heard the Lord say the minute I saw him, "Behold your son!" I literally came to a complete stand still for about thirty seconds. I could not move. It felt as if I couldn't breathe. I could not believe that I had just heard God declare this child as my son. I played the scene over and over in my head for days. I didn't even mention it to Brian right away so as not to get his hopes up if I was wrong. I knew I wasn't wrong, but I was afraid to hope in that direction.

Brian and I talked about the real chance of the family coming forward and wanting him back. At that point, we would have no choice but to turn him back over. We had heard a story or two of this happening to other missionaries. We both talked about this scenario. I remember telling Brian that if this happened, it would feel like the death of our child to us, and are we ready to take that risk? Brian, without a pause said, "YES! Yes we are." The bottom line was, if God wanted to use us this way, we would be obedient, even if we felt the loss of a child.

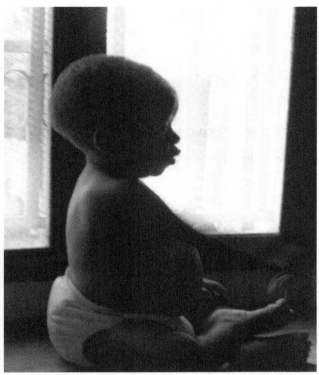

"Fat baby JoJo." He's sitting on the kitchen counter, in his cloth diaper. He always wanted to be where the food was. So, he'd sit there while I cooked.

Chapter 5

The Meeting of Mothers

"Ask and it will be given to you; seek and you will find; knock and the door will be opened to you."

-Matthew 7:7

The day was hot and not a cloud in the sky. We had taken Joseph to the baby home to play with the other kids. He loved it for the most part. It was teaching him to share and to play well with others. I remember I was in clothes that I didn't mind getting dirty and most importantly, pants that stretched. My hair was not fixed and not a single layer of makeup was on my face.

Then, the phone rang. It was the charismatic, Danish baby homeowner's wife. She had called to let me know I had about thirty minutes to prepare myself because the birth mother, grandmother, and social worker were on their way to the baby home to meet us and check on Jo. Now, come on! I waited six months for this moment, and I look like I just left the gym. And well, let's just say I'm not the gym type! This moment was a lot different in my head, and I was going to have to be okay with the "dirty gym imposter" look for our first meeting. At this point, if the family of baby Jo didn't grab him from my arms and hightail it back to the village, based on first glances, then, this was for sure a meeting set up by God.

We prayed for this meeting to happen and in true Ugandan fashion, it happened out of the blue. I was shaking to say the least. Brian was there that day and it was show time, except for the fact, I did not want to meet the family members looking like this. I had prepared mentally for what was going to take place. I think I was speed praying for the thirty, short minutes it took them to get there. When the van pulled up, we went to the driveway to meet them. I was so curious to see both these women. I was excited and scared all at once.

We stood there with the baby we knew as Joseph. He looked so different from the last time they had seen him. The baby they saw last time was emaciated and badly broken by the hands of the stepmother. This baby was on the very, healthy, chubby side and waddled when he walked. He had cheeks for days (as I like to say) and which I kissed one hundred times a day. He smiled and his eyes sparkled. He giggled when he walked and he always walked with a toy car in his hand. This was the baby he had become.

When both women stepped out of the car, I was taken with the fact that they looked like everyone else. I could tell who the grandmother was and who the mother was. The older Ugandan women always wore a Gomez, the traditional, long dress with high set shoulders we called bat wings. Her hair was wrapped in a scarf that let me know she was Muslim. Her skin was flawless and not a wrinkle in sight. I wondered if this really was the grandmother. She looked too young for that to be the case. We found out later, she was only two years older than Brian.

The person I saw next was a young, timid, Ugandan girl who looked maybe 18-20. She was beautiful, as well. She was taller than I thought she would be with a thin frame. She looked as if she was nervous and yet, very interested. We introduced ourselves and the grandmother squealed with delight. It would be another year before we found out why her reaction was so emotional and so out of character for the Ugandans. But, for today, I was so blessed by that reaction. She hugged us, but I could tell she was scanning the area for the little treasure she had truly longed to see.

We had let Joseph down, out of our arms, and he had waddled off to the play set by the time the mother and grandmother had arrived. We had to call him over to us, and we said, "This is Joseph." The social worker who had arrived with them very quickly stepped forward and said in a very thick Ugandan accent "Sudiisi" (pronounced Soo-die-see, a staunch Muslim name). The grandmother squealed and clapped with excitement, and the mother stared with a lack of emotion I could not understand. She looked at him as if she was staring at someone she once knew but couldn't place where and didn't want to get too close.

We walked inside and sat at a table where the grandmother could not take her eyes off Joseph. She said his given Muslim name over and over again. She was trying to get him to come to her, but he had no idea who she was nor had he ever responded to that name. I finally said "Joseph, come here," and he waddled right up to the table and let this woman he didn't know pick him up and place him on the table. That was a miracle. A gift from God, to the Grandmother. She touched his face and talked about how chubby he was. She touched his feet as to drink in every ounce of this sweet boy. Meanwhile, the biological mother sat emotionless, with little reaction to anything. She was interested in watching him walk around but wanted nothing else.

The social worker took control of the meeting. Our Danish friend sat with us and as she was not only the representative for the baby home but also, for us now. The mother and grandmother were told to ask as many questions as they wanted and the social worker would be the translator. The social worker explained how we came about getting Joseph which they didn't seem to mind. What they did want to know was why we changed his name. It was quickly explained the baby home manager, who was no longer employed there, renamed him. When they found out Brian and I had not done it, they were put at ease, and it showed across their faces.

The grandmother said later, in the conversation, she loved that the baby now stayed with us, but wanted to know if he could come into the village for holidays and stay with them. Panic quickly came over me, and I knew this was the most dangerous thing for him. To put him back in the baby home was one thing, but to return him to the village was completely different. I searched the face of my Danish friend and screamed inside for her to step in and reject this idea. The rejection had to come from her. We had no right to this child by law. The guardianship was granted to the baby home. Not us. Not yet, anyway.

After what seemed like forever, my friend looked at me and must have seen the horror in my face when she told the social worker that is not the best thing for the child. He is still recovering and if she would like to spend time with him, she could do so at the baby home. That put an end to the talk of him going into the village without us. I was never so grateful in my life. The conversation went on for maybe, less than an hour, and permission was granted to us, to have Joseph live in our house, as long as we wanted. We were going to have to go before the judge to be granted permission to foster him though.

As we were getting up to leave, the social worker said to Brian, "Give it some time, but she is going to consent to the adoption." We were shocked. We were only coming to meet them, not thinking a major step would take place. The mother had already lost her parental rights so, the permission for the adoption fell on the grandmother and the Muslim village. After the meeting, the grandmother was so full of joy, she hugged us as she got in the van to leave. The mother gave us a slight smile. We left with a promise of being called to the village and the rest was up to God.

Chapter 6

Man Says No, but God Said Yes

"For no matter how many promises God has made, they are "Yes" in Christ. And so through him the "Amen" is spoken by us to the glory of God."

-2 Corinthians 1:20

We waited over three months for the phone to ring, as we were living off the promise from the social worker. When the Grandmother was ready, she would call us into the village to meet the family. During that time, we hounded our friends and family on social media to pray for the adoption to be granted and for us to be able to walk out this journey with strength and grace. It was at this time, we had to go to Kampala, one of our many trips to the immigration office.

As we stood in the long lines, in the blaring heat, we met a fellow American missionary, with the Nazarene Church, which happened to be the denomination Brian grew up in and sparked up a great conversation. They talked for what seemed like an hour. It was an instant friendship. By the end of the conversation, they swapped contact info and the man said, "If we ever drive through Masaka, we will call you." Well, people say that every day. We never expected to see them again...until we did.

A few months later, the phone rang, and it was our sweet, fellow American Nazarene missionary, from the immigration office. He said he and his wife would be traveling through town and would love to stop and have lunch with us. We were so excited! We were hungry for people who knew where we came from. We missed conversation we didn't have to "explain." They would understand all of our jokes and my speedy accent. We quickly got ready and drove down the little dirt road to the Danish Café. We recognized them as soon as they walked up. We had never met his wife, but we all seemed to look alike. I knew they must be the Americans.

They were such a sweet, seasoned missionary couple. We asked them how long they had been in Uganda, to which they told us, twenty-five years. I think we had to pick our chins up off the table. Ugandan living was hard. I mean really hard! For the people who come for two to four weeks at a time, they have no idea the warfare that goes on, on a daily basis. For the people who come to STAY, it's like nothing we were ever ready for.

Staying twenty-five years was dumbfounding. They were instant heroes in our book. We picked their brains for all the tips they could give us. We sat back and soaked everything in. If they were here for twenty-five years, then, they knew how to live here, and we needed to know too. We shared stories about our kids and life before Uganda. Brian and I drank up everything they said. We had missed hearing our own American accent, coming from other people, something that had never crossed our minds. We told them our journey with Joseph, and what we were in the middle of.

The wife listened very politely to the whole story and then began to speak, "I have been here for twenty-five years. I have seen this story play out countless times. You need to prepare yourselves. You are a Christian. The Muslims don't ever give their children to Christians. Even though, they kicked him out of the village, they will take him back, just to keep you from having him. If the birth family doesn't have the money to raise him, the village will pull all their money together and go before a judge to convince them otherwise. The bottom line, they will never agree to this and they will never give you their permission."

I sat there and listened as she sincerely shared what she has seen in the past twenty-five years. I remember listening and not feeling phased by it at all. Not one negative emotion crept in. It bounced off of me as if there was something in front of me. As she was speaking, I kept thinking about the Lord saying, "Behold your son." I know He said that to me! When she finished her story, I looked at her, with peace in my heart and voice, and I told her my story. I told her just what God had said to me, that day in the kitchen. I said to her, "The Muslims may not want to give me their child, but God told me he was my son, so I have no doubt they will sign the papers. God said, "BEHOLD YOUR SON." "He's our son." I said it with joy and confidence and never doubted it wouldn't be. I didn't know how God would do it, but I never doubted he was ours from that day forward.

A couple of months later, the phone rang, and it was the social worker from the baby home, telling us the grandmother was ready for us to come. I remember getting JoJo dressed in his best, little summer outfit and telling him that we were going to the village to see his Jaja (grandmother). Of course, he had no idea what that meant, but it made me feel better knowing I prepared him the best I could. Before we made the hour drive to the village of Menzy, we stopped and picked up our Danish friend and her social worker Brenda.

Chapter 7

Why Emeralds?

"The Lord their God will save His people on that day as a shepherd saves his flock. They will sparkle in his land like jewels in a crown."

-Zechariah 9:16

Have you ever had a moment with God, in your prayer time, that seemed as if He had taken you to a quiet, still place where just you and He could have a moment? Well, that's how my prayer time would be from time to time and more often than not.

The scene always played out in a castle type setting where I was in a beautiful ball gown, waiting for my prince to show up and spin me on the dance floor. I'm such a princess, even in my prayer time. For over a year, this played out, and every time Jesus would show up, He had a black, velvet box with a piece of stunning jewelry in it. Man, God was making sure my time with Him got my attention. Princess dresses and jewelry are my love languages! The jewelry would always be some sort of emerald. I didn't know why it was always emeralds. I began to say, "God, I really appreciate it. Each piece of jewelry I'm given is stunning, but why emeralds?" I know what you are thinking...I'm crazy! God is handing me jewelry and I'm wanting a different color. Yeah, not my coolest moment. Green was never a color I would pick, and I was more of a diamond girl. But, He never answered my question. I knew it meant something, but not even Google could give me the answer I was looking for (and yes, I did Google).

***

I'm not sure what time of day he took his first breath or how much he weighed. I'm not sure how long he measured. I'm not even sure if it was day or night. I'm not sure if his cheeks were stroked with love or if he was held in awe. I'm not sure who soothed his first cries or gave him his first bath. What I do know is, the One who knit him together in the womb knows. I know He breathed life into his lungs. He knew his weight, his length, his time of birth. HE held him. He soothed his first cries. He stroked his cheeks in love and HE held this baby boy with awe and wonder. He was His creation and He was ecstatic about this one. This baby was wanted by his Creator. This baby was created for greatness! Not one day of his life has been overlooked by the ONE who wanted him most.

***

We sat in a two-room house made of concrete. The ceilings were so unfinished that the rafters were exposed. We were deep in a Muslim village. As I sat there, I looked into the face of a young mother, who was a teenager when she gave birth to that baby boy. I knew our lives would always be connected. My heart would always be grateful for the gift she gave us. We began to ask her questions about the day he was born. In Uganda, it's possible for one to never truly know the actual day they were born. We asked in hopes that by some chance she would actually know. We were told at the baby home that the staff thought his birthday was in July and there would never be a way of really knowing. We were told we could just pick a day in July and make that his birthday. I understood the concept but was never really comfortable with that idea. I loved this baby just like all of my birth children. I wanted to know when my son was born.

With hope and apprehension, I took a deep breath and looked her in the eyes and asked, "Do you know on what day he was born?" She looked at me, without hesitation, and said, "May 9, 2009, it was a Tuesday." She quickly put her head down and was silent again. Without warning, in my mind, I instantly saw the black box that God had presented to me for over the past year. It opened once more! I could not move and this time it was empty. I could not blink and no one knew I was having a moment with God that was so much bigger than I ever thought possible. After a year of asking Him, "Why emeralds?"

He took my hand one last time in a little concrete house as I was looking into the face of my son's birth mother and said, as if to say, "This is 'WHY EMERALDS.'" I had no clue the emeralds were the precious stones of my new son's birth! I couldn't breathe. For over a year, God had been preparing me for the most precious and rare gift. No wonder He didn't tell me a year ago. He knew I would have laughed just like Sarah when He told me that one day, I would find myself in a Muslim village, meeting the family of the child I was about to adopt. Or, He didn't tell me for the fact I'm known to be a runner and would have Jonah'd my way right out of His plan.

The box was empty this time, which didn't have any effect on me, until I sat down to write this book. Empty for the first time in a year, my little treasure was sitting next to me on his daddy's lap. The place where he began to trust and feel safe again. There was no need for emeralds this time. This was the moment God had prepared me for. My treasure was flesh and blood, and God knew I would need that confirmation when the Deceiver came hissing his lies about the fact this adoption would never take place. Never again would I second guess that Joseph was ours.

It was during my little "heart attack" with the Lord that Brian looked back in his calendar on his phone to verify, if indeed, May 9, 2009, was a Tuesday, and it was. There it was. The answer I so desperately wanted. God is the only one who knew I would walk away with the answers to so many questions my heart had been yearning to know that day. I wonder if, as I woke up that day, if God was pacing back and forth in anticipation for that moment. I wonder if He felt like a parent on Christmas morning waiting for their kids to wake up to a room full of goodies, wrapped tenderly with love? I mean, for the past year He had been giving me hints of what my gift was. But what am I thinking? He invented Christmas! As I looked into the face of this mother, my heart swelled with gratitude. I wanted to run to her and put my arms around her and thank her for the most precious gift we could ever be given.

On one side of the room was a young teenage mother, surrounded by her family and local villagers. The very people who had kicked her and her newborn son out of the village. All because she was an unwed, Muslim mother, who had become the "Scarlet Letter," to her people. On the other side of the room, there was a seasoned mother and father who had fallen in love, unexpectedly, with a baby who was desperately in need of a family.

As we sat there, I knew we were watching history in the making. I had never forgotten what our missionary friends told us months earlier, "The Muslim community never gives up their own to a Christian." (Anyone who is white is considered a Christian).

The day was hot and dry. The room heaved with family members and local villagers. They could not believe this was the same child from two years ago. The grandmother (who was only 45 at the time of our meeting) told us that this boy had been born sick. She said her and her own mother did what they could to keep him alive. Through the translator, she explained the baby had been born yellow and not well. I told her it was more than likely what's called jaundice. And if she ever had another grandchild that was born that way again, she could lay them naked, in the sun, for 5 to 10 minutes a few times a day to help with that situation. She was very pleased with this information.

Our translator, Brenda, went on to tell us the man in the corner was LC. This was the modern name for the village chief. He is the one person in the village that has the power to okay the adoption and sign the birth certificate. He stepped forward and looked at us and said the following, "I am the LC of this village. I am also this boy's uncle. I am very pleased to give you this child as your son. On this day, I will fill out the birth certificate. We would like, at this time, to give this child your name, but we only ask two things of you. We ask you to keep the family name somewhere in his new name, and we also ask you to get him circumcised." This was to protect him from the local witchdoctors.

At this point, the LC, Joseph's uncle, went on to say, the family and village was honored we wanted to take this child and raise him to manhood. He told us they had seen many white people come to Uganda to give occasional aid to the children of their country, but never had they seen two people come and love a child that was not their own, willing to provide for him until adulthood. They were honored and blessed by our actions, which they confessed, they could not understand. They could not possibly understand how we could love a child that was not our own. They proceeded to tell us if we were willing to do this, then they were ready as a village to put him into our hands.

Months later, we came to understand, through our translator, that at this first meeting, we should have been killed, and it would have been perfectly acceptable. We were told, Christians are not allowed to come into that village, and if we did, we were to be killed before we left. We not only came that hot July day, but we came two more times before we left Uganda, greeted with a celebration every time.

They always prepared food for us, and we ate with them. They were so surprised that we wanted to eat our meal with them as they said, "Who are these people that they would want to eat with us?" Those words still break my heart. If I could step back in time, I would look them in the face and tell them, "You are the family of my new son. I will always sit at your table. I will always love you, and you are our family now."

Joseph's uncle is signing the adoption papers. He is the village Chief. His is filling out his birth certificate. In order to get the OFFICIAL birth certificate, we had to have the "chief's signature."

Me (Angela), Brian, and Joseph, right after the Chief gave permission to adopt.

Chapter 8

Family Ties

"In their hearts humans plan their course, but the Lord establishes their steps."

-Proverbs 16:9

Mickdard - biological father

He was born into the most committed Muslim family. His family tree includes men who had made the pilgrimage to Mecca. I have seen with my own eyes some of the poorest villages in Uganda. Making a trip all the way to Saudi Arabia couldn't have been an easy one for them. But if you end up being one of the village's lucky ones, to make that pilgrimage, you come back to win the prestige of the local village and all the benefits that go with it. I believe he grew up seeing what it meant to be that privileged member of the village, but financially would not be able to achieve it. I also believe he searched for ways to reach the highest status he could without actually making that trip.

Somewhere on Mickdard's journey, he met Aisha, a very young girl who wanted to be loved and pursued. She was also raised in a very traditional Muslim village. She knew the risk of a forbidden relationship and was willing to pay the price. It wasn't long before Mickdard and Aisha were expecting a child. Aisha would end up paying that price and Mickdard would continue to climb the ladder of honor in the Muslim community. It was a year or so later when Mickdard would receive a visitor that would change his life in a very big and surprising way.

Aisha had found her way to him and gave him the baby he had planned to leave with her. We were told that it's a Muslim mans goal, or some would even say, duty, to make as many children as possible. This child Aisha was delivering to him made number six for him. He may have been surprised to see the baby on his doorstep, but it would not make any difference to him. He would leave and travel for work. Mickdard would leave this baby with his current wife and new son and not return for weeks at a time. Every time he would come home, this baby's physical condition would be worse, but it still would make no difference to him. He hoped with all his heart this child would not survive the conditions he was being subject to, but he underestimated the strength bottled up in this tiny body and the plans God had for this wee one.

***

Aisha - biological mother

Aisha grew up in a tiny Muslim village called Nenzy, off the beaten path in southern Uganda. To find her village you would have to know it was there. It wasn't a place known by anyone but the locals. She wasn't just any girl of the village. Aisha was the niece of the village chief. From birth, she would have been taught exactly what was expected of her. She was required to live a spotless life so as not to bring embarrassment to the "royal" family.

As a girl, she went to school. For us in the west, that seems like no big deal, but for families in Uganda, that was not a luxury afforded to every child. From what we were told, she did attend up to high school, but what that actually means or how far she made it, will remain a mystery. Aisha was a free spirit. She knew what was expected but had her own plans. She wasn't one to be held back by the rules of the village leaders or her religion. Exactly when Mickdard came into the picture is unknown as well. What is known is he pursued her with a passion she was drawn to. She knew the risk, but was willing to take that chance. She was hoping not to be just another notch in his belt, but would soon find out she was just another girl used to climb the ladder of success.

Nothing is known of her pregnancy or when Mickdard left, but the facts show he did leave, forcing her to enter parenthood on her own, to deliver this child, with the help of her mother and grandmother. From the moment her baby was born, it was nothing but heartache and stress. He was born weak and discolored which was surely viewed as a curse. The village was turned upside down because now the village chief had an unwed teenage mother for a niece.

Months passed and the baby grew and became healthier. I can't imagine how it was to live in a village that truly believed she had become the "Scarlet Letter". In her culture, she had brought shame on the family's name, and there was nothing else her father could do to clear it but to banish her and the child from ever returning to the village. The day she left, she knew exactly where to go and what to do. The only one who was devastated about their leaving was her own mother, Rehema. Aisha took the next bus to Masaka and would soon deliver the child back to the man who had left her to face the hardship and shame all on her own.

**

Rehema - maternal grandmother

She is the sister-in-law of the village chief. She is Aisha's mother. And thanks to Aisha, is a first-time grandmother. A title she loves wholeheartedly. The first thing you notice about Rehema is her smile. This smile lights up an entire room. It's a sight I will never forget. She is loved by all who know her. She loves and rocks on her lap every child that gets near her. Rehema's name in Arabic means kind and compassionate. I can think of no other name more fitting for a person. Her personality was not reserved in any way. She found exploding joy in every situation. Her laughter filled the atmosphere and infected every person within earshot of her voice. Just one of the many things you can say about her is she loves and loves well.

The people at the top of her list are her own family, but she also loves her community, with the same passion.

When I met her in the village, I could tell her role was the mother and grandmother of the entire village. She was surrounded by people that loved and highly respected her. When she is excited, she screams with joy, which brings people running in from the fields. I have seen this happen with my own eyes.

The day her first grandchild was born, I have no doubt she held him tightly in her arms. Her smile and joy were the first he would have ever seen or felt. When she realized this child was not well, she and her own mother took on the responsibility of his medical care. They would toil day and night for this sweet child she loved fiercely. For Rehema, there was no other way to love. She was not blind to the drama and unfortunate cultural stain that this new life brought with it. She was wise beyond her years and knew in the end what she too would have to give up. The day her daughter and grandson were forced to leave, hot tears were streaming down her face. She prayed silently as they walked out of sight.

Left to right: Rehema, Joseph, with his grandfather, holding him. He is also Rehema's husband. The young lady standing on the right is Joseph's birth mother, Aisha. Notice the faces. Joseph did not want his grandfather holding him. By this time, Aisha had been kicked out of the village but, by law, she had to be there for the adoption, therefore, she had to be tracked down.

Chapter 9

Scaling Mt. Paperwork

"Let us not become weary in doing good, for at the proper time we will reap a harvest if we do not give up."

-Galatians 6:9

After the meeting in the village, which led to the signing of the birth certificate, we sat and enjoyed a long, deep breath. We learned along the way there were so many ins and outs to this international adoption. All the different legs of this race we had yet to run. Just when we crossed one hurdle, there would be another one waiting for us.

We are beyond thankful for all the people God put in our path, to encourage us along the way. Without them, we surely would have wilted. We were surrounded by a strong mission's community. They became our family for the 2 years we lived there. I'm so thankful for their love, friendship, and wisdom they poured into us on a weekly basis. Even now, as I write this, the joy we shared can still be felt, and I would give anything to hug all of our friends from Denmark, Canada, the UK, Belgium, the United States, and Greece. They need to know that the community they gave us is more precious to us than we have words to tell them.

As I look back, I see the hand of God in every relationship we had in Masaka. One such family just so happened to be from Florida. Liv and Tyler were a young couple who had been to Masaka before and actually, had gone through a Ugandan adoption a few years prior. This time they had returned to start a project, still changing lives in Uganda today.

As we got to know Liv and Tyler, we walked them through our journey with Joseph. Liv was able to fill me in on all that was still left to do. It was so overwhelming, I wondered how we would actually achieve our goal of one day taking Joseph home to America. I can tell you "how" is God's job. Trusting Him is ours. That became my motto for the rest of this journey. Every time we faced a roadblock, I would let these words wash over my weary bones.

One of the surprising things required of us, was to have an American home study done in Uganda, just like we were adopting in the US. Thanks to Liv and Tyler also going through their second Ugandan adoption, they already knew the perfect person for the job. Sharon had already been to Uganda a few years back for this very reason. We felt very excited to have a social worker who was very familiar with this process. I almost felt like I could take a deep breath and pause for a moment (but just for a moment).

The phone rang in late January, and it was Liv on the other end asking if we wanted to split the airfare to get the social worker to Uganda. Without hesitation, I said, "YES!" And just like that the tickets were bought. She would be here February 25, 2013, and another leg of the journey had begun.

As we began to talk to our U.S. social worker, Sharon, through email, I realized the amount of work still left to be done. It was going to make us facing a Muslim village feel like a cake walk. She sent us endless forms that had to be filled out, and there were still requirements we had to pass in order for the U.S. government to okay this adoption. One of which was, meeting the financial requirement to adopt a child. What? We were missionaries, so I doubted it, but I found myself saying, "Yes," and trusting God to make money appear where it needed to. The next thing she needed was proof that we did make said money. That made the blood drain from my veins because I was certain in the last year there was no way we made the money needed to make this baby ours. I sent word to a few friends asking them to pray God would work out this hurdle. It would be a parting of the Red Sea type miracle, but we were familiar with those types of miracles and were certain this would be no different.

As the deadline approached for us to submit our first stack of forms (the ones that would prove we were financially stable enough to pursue this adoption), Brian poured over our financial records. I remember the sound of relief that came from Brian as he hit the last key on the laptop. He said, "Come over here and see this." As I leaned over his shoulder, I knew the moment had arrived. Depending on this number, it would mean our journey had come to an end or we got to push on. As I looked at the screen, I saw we were over by a few hundred dollars. We not only qualified, but we were over the amount needed. My next words, "HOW?" We had only ten financial supporters who joined us on this journey. We not only qualified, but we overqualified. I won't reveal the amount needed, but know, this had just turned into our "Red Sea" miracle or that moment Jesus sent his disciples to catch a fish, and when they opened its mouth inside, they found the money they needed to pay their taxes! Yep! This was that moment in real time. God will make a way, and He usually does it when all other ways are gone, so that there is no other explanation but for His glory. I quickly sent word and forms to our U.S. social worker that we would definitely be continuing with the process.

We just want to thank everyone involved for helping us with this part of our story. Some of our friends had to write reference letters. Some of our family had to track down and mail marriage certificates, birth certificates, and tax forms. This was not a lonely journey. We had a crew of people helping us behind the scenes to make this sweet baby ours. We will forever be grateful for the part you played in our story.

Joseph's very first visit to Queen Elizabeth National Park.

Chapter 10

The Social Worker Has Landed

"When you are brought before synagogues, rulers and authorities, do not worry about how you will defend yourselves or what you will say, for the Holy Spirit will teach you at that time what you should say."

-Luke 12:11

The day was February 25, 2013. A thin layer of clouds made the sky gray, but there was no way the gray day would affect the excitement buzzing around our house. We had spent days preparing our house and ourselves for this moment. We had also, without doubt, spent hours in prayer for this home study. Liv did her best to explain to us what our home study interview would be like, but we still had no idea what it would be like for us.

The moment arrived and our big, green gates at the bottom of our driveway opened with the familiar squeak from the dried-out hinges. We saw Liv and Tyler's van pull

97

up, and we went out to greet them. Liv made the introductions, and we were greeted by the most amazing, warm smile from Sharon, our American social worker. Thanks to such a peaceful, loving presence about her, our nerves were instantly calmed, and all fear slipped away. We assured Liv and Tyler we would drop her back off at their house when we were done. They quickly pulled out of our driveway, and we walked inside, talking at the speed only Americans understood. We were so happy to have another fellow American at our house, if only for a few hours.

Sharon quickly took the lead, saying, "Tell me your story. The story of how you got Joseph." We started from the beginning and told her of everything we could think. I'm sure I left no detail out because when I tell stories, I seem to paint a complete picture, setting the scene so you actually feel like you are there. I just like to tell a story in High Def. I'm all about quality. I can't say Brian is a big fan of my story telling. Bless his heart. He's more of a bullet point guy, but with over twenty years of marriage, he has learned to just sit back and enjoy the ride. I knew with great detail this story was going to have to be told. I can't say that's why our interview lasted for five hours, but Sharon seemed to feel that the length in which ours took was the norm.

During this time, she dove into family history and relationships with relatives. She asked very detailed and sometimes difficult but, needed questions, about our childhoods and took notes as we told her our life story. She got up and took the usual tour around the house to make sure Joseph had a bed of his own. She also made sure we had a bathroom with running water (she came on a good day because it actually came on when she turned on the faucet), a fire extinguisher, and all medications were out of his reach. She then, asks to speak to Emily and Morgan, our second and third born children. We were asked to leave the room while she conducted the sibling part of the interview. It didn't take long as she sat and listened to them share their hearts and feelings on the thought of adopting a little brother, even to the point of asking Morgan if he was okay giving up his title of "baby of the family," to this new little one. Morgan with all his Morgan gusto answered a very assured, "YES!"

When we were called back in, she had a few final questions for us and then said, "You really do have a miracle story with a miracle boy. I will be recommending to the U.S. government that you be allowed to move forward with the adoption." I don't think I blinked for ten seconds. When my eyelids did begin to work again, I'm sure I squealed with all my might. We had just jumped another hurdle and were running full speed to the finish line. There was still so much to be done in this adoption, and we were unaware of what was still to come.

I think I ran on pure joy for a few days, following our home study, so when it came time to print off a ten, page application to be sent to the U.S. Embassy in Nairobi, Kenya, it didn't faze me. We had waited a little over a month for Sharon to send official documents of the U.S. Home Study to Uganda. We would need to put a packet of application papers and passport pictures together to send to the embassy in Kenya. That's where the main embassy was for the U.S.

Unfortunately, during that time, in Nairobi, there was a presidential election taking place. The previous election that was held there ended up being very violent and shutting down the city for some time. We were told by the Embassy, if that did happen, our paperwork would be put on hold and the whole process could be lost all together. We prayed so hard, as did our prayer support in the U.S., during Kenya's election. Never before did we have so much personally at stake when it came to another country's election! We watched and waited for the election to come and go. It was a peaceful event. We knew our packet was safe.

My favorite thing about the Kenya Embassy process was we were able to give our email address to them and when we were approved by the U.S. government to proceed to adopt Joseph, they would send word. In Uganda, we had no idea where we were in any of the process. We were kept in the dark much of the time, both literally and figuratively. So, to have the reassurance we would be contacted in the end provided so much peace.

I don't remember how long we waited to get that email, but it wasn't longer than a month. I saw the heading in the message line and knew it was from Nairobi. I quickly opened it, reading, Joseph was declared an orphan and therefore, considered adoptable by the U.S. government. There it was, permission from our government, to move forward in adopting our boy.

We had stood before a Muslim village, who gladly gave us their child, when others said it would not be done. We were granted permission from our own county, as our packet miraculously escaped a potential political war. Now, before us, was our greatest battle. We had no idea what was against us in the shadows of Uganda, but we now had to turn and face another country, asking them to trust us enough to hand over their fellow countryman, allowing him to be raised an American.

This is our big, iron, squeaky gate.

Produce stand, down the street from our home. The big, oval shaped things on the ground are called Jack Fruit. They fall from a tree and they will kill.

Chapter 11

Rats Ate Our Paperwork

"For see, today I have made you strong like a fortified city that cannot be captured, like an iron pillar or a bronze wall. You will stand against the whole land – the kings, officials, priests and people of Judah. They will fight you, but they will fail for I am with you and I will take care of you."

-Jeremiah 1:18-19

Nothing in Uganda moves fast. For us Americans, it's as painful as pulling our hair out one by one. We are so used to timely responses and schedules that are kept because you have important official jobs. We are used to getting official documents back from attorney's offices that usually aren't half eaten by rats. When we have court dates, we are used to having the judge show up because it's their job. Well, none of our cultural rules apply in

Uganda, and yes, rats did eat our paperwork that was left in our attorney's office. And when the Judge decided to finally come to work, she was very mad our attorney presented her with such horrible documents. The crazy thing about this story, the portion that was eaten away was the birth mother's signature which was needed as proof that she agreed to this adoption. The judge allowed them, in spite of their condition, but it just goes to show you the lengths Satan went to, to stop our process.

We came to understand a few things called "African Time" or TIA (This Is Africa). It was the most frustrating thing I had ever experienced. I would tell Brian, almost daily, "What takes one or two steps in the western world takes four in Africa." It was all the extra steps that were killing me. We had to make the three hour drives back and forth to Kampala, the Ugandan capital, on several occasions, needlessly. I look back on it now and truly believe it was the enemy's attempt to wear us down. It was so close to working if it weren't for DOB: all the prayer.

God had sent us lifelines along our adoption process way. We had Liv and Tyler who lived ten minutes away, and, as I said, they were fellow Americans adopting while living in Uganda. We also had another family who we had known from being on the same team with us when we first landed in Uganda named David and Nita Loveall, a pastor and wife couple from Oregon that we have come to love. Nita was the first of the Lovealls to step foot in Uganda. While she was there, she met William, who was the most amazing, thirteen-year-old Ugandan boy. He was at one of the local boarding schools we were closely working with. By the time the team was ready to leave, she had fallen hard for William. Nita had made him a promise in which she would be back for him. It wasn't long when Nita and her husband, David, pulled into our driveway and the loud American squeals began!

We fell in love with David and Nita right away. We were meeting David for the first time and right from the start, I loved this guy. He was loud and outgoing. He had a smile that would light up any dark room. He was hilarious and if there was anything lacking during that season of life, it was laughter. Within the first hour of meeting David, I saw a soft sensitive side of him that melted our hearts. When Nita left the first time, we didn't have Joseph yet, and when she returned, there was a little Ugandan baby living in our house calling us "mom and dad". We quickly told them the story of Joseph and the how and why he ended up living with us. I looked up to find tears rolling down their faces and that's when it hit us. We really did have a miraculous story that would not only impact us but everyone we told.

We didn't know it then, but Nita would have to return home for work, and David would end up staying with us for three months in order to fulfill her promise to William, of bringing him back to the U.S.A. If it hadn't been for David and Nita going through this process, a few steps before us, we would have been blindsided and lost a lot along the way. God used them in a mighty way, not only for William, but for the Rowe family, as well. We will always be grateful for them and the way our adoption stories intersected in Uganda.

As I write this, I can't stop smiling, thinking back through all the shenanigans the Rowe and Loveall family got into to help pass the time and bring joy to our very, heavy, uncertain journeys. When the adoption finally got approved, I gave him a giant American flag and told him to wave it loud and proud when he finally got home. I also said, "We are right behind you." I will always treasure the memories of our Katwe days.

Chapter 12

TICK...TICK...TICK

"Consider it pure joy, my brothers and sisters, whenever you face trials of many kinds, because you know that the testing of your faith produces perseverance. Let perseverance finish its work so that you may be mature and complete, not lacking anything."

-James 1:2-4

We waited and waited for the phone to ring and the dates to be set. We received our clearance from the Embassy in Kenya, and thought doors would start opening, but to our surprise, they didn't.

We knew we would need to hire an attorney to continue this legal battle and thanks to the Loveall family, we knew right where to go. We were able to hire the same one they used. He was a fantastic man, but a little nervous at practicing family law. I stopped to ask what kind of lawyer he was, due to little glitches I had noticed. His reply was, "Land title attorney." I just slapped my forehead and thought this is going to make a great book.

He had assured us, besides the Loveall family, there had been other families who had hired him to do this very thing. I asked him how many cases he had won. He told me every case he took before the family court had ended in victory. That brought me some comfort. In that moment, we looked at each other and knew we were a motley crew, but God usually takes the road less traveled with us or the most unlikely people to accomplish the most extraordinary things. This turn of events would be no different.

Our attorney started to build his case, asking us to go to the police station and request the police file. We thought that would be drama free, but why? Why did we think that? We walked in and saw a policewoman sitting behind a very, disheveled desk. It was piled high with papers and folders. We were in the department of family welfare. She looked up at us from behind the pile and we introduced ourselves. When we told her who we were, she looked at us like she had seen a ghost.

We explained we were in need of the police records belonging to Joseph. She quickly went to her desk drawer and pulled out a picture of a very, well-kept Ugandan couple. She then told us, "This is the birth father of the boy you are speaking of. He has been looking for him for months and wants him back. In fact, when you leave here, I will be calling him and letting him know you people have been found, and where he can retrieve his son from." Fear mixed with anger filled my entire body. I don't know who spoke first, Brian or me. When the dust settled, what was conveyed to her was that he would never get his son back for the fact of nearly ending his life! She had tried to deliver the final punch with what she said next, "I'm calling the social worker. You won't get this boy. His father wants him back."

We walked out mad, but more determined than ever before to protect this sweet child from any more abuse. We had a couple of thoughts as we got back into the car. First, how did she have that picture of the family at the top of her desk drawer, ready to shove at us when we walked into the office? The initial rescue and arrest happened over two years ago. It was like, she knew we would be coming. And second, why did she look like she had seen a ghost when she saw us?

We left the police station and headed straight to the social workers office. To our great surprise, she was there. That was an absolute miracle. This woman was never in her office. Brian and I walked in and asked to speak to her. We were taken back to her office and quickly told her what had taken place. She let us know she would never allow that man to have Joseph back, due to the conditions in which he left him. She told us the policewoman was just trying to scare us for some reason, and was sure the father NEVER wanted Joseph back. She said for us not to worry and she would make some phone calls. We left the office in a little better state of mind than when we walked in.

Unfortunately, we were no closer in our quest than when the day started. We knew the only person who could get the police file would be our attorney. We got home and called him explaining what had taken place. He told us he could be in Masaka in a few days to help with the situation. We made arrangements for him to make the three hour trip south to get the ball rolling. Within a few days, he was there, just like he said. We picked him up from the bus stop and he requested we take him to the police station right away. As we pulled in, he asked Brian and me to stay in the car and not get out.

He was in there for about thirty minutes. As he got in the car, he said, "I have the file, but I must ask you, who is "Linda" (this is not her actual name)?" I said, "How do you know who that is?" He then told us the conversation he just had with the same policewoman we had talked to a few days earlier. "Linda" had done everything she could to keep us from being able to adopt Joseph. Our attorney told us for over a year she had put a stop to any of the process going forward. "Linda" had gone to people in high places telling them we would be coming to adopt Joseph and should stop us at all cost.

The officials were told we were unfit and even abusive towards him. The policewoman said she was told what to say to us if we ever showed up and that's how she had the picture at the top of her drawer. The police also told our attorney they had followed us for a year to see if the allegations against us were true. After a year of following us, they could see we loved the child and never did him any harm. The attorney was just as shocked as we were to learn of this story. He could hardly believe it was true.

I will say, at that moment, everything came flooding back. All the starts and stops, all the cancelled appointments, all the times the Ugandan social worker could not be reached, and so on. To this day, this portion of our story remains a mystery. We have no idea what this person had to gain from stopping our adoption. I could sit and speculate, but that does me no good. The only thing I know for sure is, what God wants to happen will happen!

"...They will fight you but will not win."

Mother's Day, May 2013, in the front yard of our house.
Joseph randomly came up behind me and hugged me.
Funny side note: The "shed" behind us, with three doors,
are out houses. We DID NOT use those! We had a
bathroom in the house. Well, only the boys, when the
other was occupied. They loved it!

Chapter 13

Call Your Embassy

"When you pass through the waters, I will be with you; and when you pass through the rivers, they will not sweep over you. When you walk through the fire, you will not be burned; the flames will not set you ablaze."

-Isaiah 43:2

The things we learned on the mission field ended up being things that could never be learned in a classroom. They were things that could only be taught to us by living and submerging ourselves into the culture of Uganda. Ugandan people are beautiful, loving people. They are hardworking and for the most part, take pride in what they do. That being said, we did come across a few exceptions as one would in any country and in any corner of the world.

We worked with a beautiful couple at the boarding school we had partnered with. Kassim was the sweetest

Muslim man we had met there. His wife, Prossy, was just as lovely. Together, they were the Headmasters (similar to principal) of the school. Brian worked very closely with them, almost, on a daily basis. Brian and Kassim would sit at our house going over the monthly budget for what seemed like hours. Kassim's heart was for those kids of the school. He also kept the teachers very close to his heart, as he knew they didn't have a school without them. Over a year, Brian worked closely with him, trying to make ends meet and making the financial support stretch as far as it would go. They had forged an unlikely friendship that Brian still finds as an unforgettable blessing. Brian tells people there were only about five people in Uganda he could wholeheartedly trust and Kassim was at the top.

One day, Kassim came to our house looking very upset, asking to speak to us outside, away from our children. We went to the front yard and set up chairs under a shade tree where he spoke the words I will never forget, "It's time to call your embassy." Brian and I looked at each other, looked back at him, and asked the obvious, "Why?" He said, "I have gotten word that there are some people who are going to try to kill you, and you shouldn't go back up to the school. You are not safe, and neither are we."

We sat there in absolute shock. We knew the ones they were referring to, and apparently, we had upset them by coming to Uganda to manage control of the finances for the organization. It meant the mishandling of the money stopped with us and these people would no longer be able to skim off the top. AND that's being polite. The village that surrounded the school had come to tell Kassim and Prossy of the devious plan. The village also told this beautiful couple they should not eat at the school because the plan was to poison them. They took this warning very seriously, and the first thing they did was come to tell us.

One Sunday evening, we all sat on the couch to watch a movie. Sounds like no big deal, but to us, it was very special because we weren't sure when the electricity would go out. As we were getting ready to settle in with our popcorn and our special feature, I had a very, slight nudge to lock the screen door. We had learned to listen to that small still voice and just obey. I didn't know why I felt that, but I knew I was to listen. We had kept the door open and unlocked in the evenings because our cat would come and go until it was time to lock the house up for the night. We never felt unsafe. We lived behind a nine-foot-tall concrete wall, but on this night, I thought, "Oh well, if she wants in, I will just get up and let her in."

About halfway through the movie, Brian got up to go to the kitchen and the next thing we heard made our hearts stop. All of a sudden, Brian screamed, "Grab the machete!" We all jumped as fast as we could and ran to the front of the house where Brian's voice had come from. Morgan was the first to the kitchen to grab it. Brian kept yelling, "There were men by the door who were trying to get in!" Unbeknownst to us, while we were watching the movie, two men circled the house to try to sneak in and ambush us.

They had tried every window and had made it to the screen door when Brian had gotten up. They were trying to get in when Brian reached the door and caught them in the act. Brian chased them to the back of the house where they scaled that nine-foot wall with ease, while Brian was yelling at them. The men were over the wall, but on top of the hill behind our house. They knew Brian had the machete when they began pleading with Brian to not kill them, even though, Brian was still on the other side of the wall.

Brian was yelling and demanding to know who they were. One of the men yelled back, "We were sent here tonight by the man you work for." Brian responded, "We don't work for anyone here." "Yes, you do," said the man and continued, "He sent us here tonight to harm you and your family." Brian asked him for a name. The man told him he could not tell, but assured Brian we knew exactly who it was. Brian yelled, "I'm going to find you!" And the men sprinted away in the dark. Brian never found them but wasn't for lack of trying. I shake to think what would have happened if I had not taken that one second to flip the latch on the door to lock it.

Needless to say, we were pretty shaken for a while after that. I called home and told my mom what we had just been through. My poor mom! She was left helpless and scared. It really did a number on her, and I should have rethought my plan. The one thing it did do was produce prayer. She called everyone she knew, including the State Department. From my understanding, my uncle made that same call to the State Department. They rallied the troops where people began to pray for our safety. Now, the State Department had to deal with two phone calls that had come in about an American family who had their life threatened in Uganda.

The threats did not stop there. Sometime later, a man tried to break into our house in the middle of the night, and Brian just so happened to be awake the whole night. Had he been asleep, he would have never heard the breaking of the padlock which caused him to run to the door, just in time, to see a man inside our door. The man ran away before Brian could reach him. It was a good thing because I know with all we had gone through, it would not have ended well for this guy.

The final threat came not long before we left. We had hired a "Head of Security" for our housing compound. His name is Thomas. He is a Kenyan who we came to love dearly while we were there. He said men had come to him asking about being guards, specifically, for the Mzungu house (our house). Being a dear trusted friend, he questioned them until getting to the bottom of their asking.

The day was hot, and the sun was shining high in the sky. I heard the familiar squeaking of the gates and ran to the screen door to see Thomas coming in. I greeted him in the front yard. He said, "My dear, I must tell you not to let JoJo out in the yard to play by himself." My smile from the greeting quickly faded away with his words. He continued, "Men have come to me asking to guard your house with the sole purpose of stealing JoJo." They said the child belongs to one of their sisters and they plan on giving him back.

Thomas was a smart man. He asked what village their sister was from, and it was not the same as where

Joseph was born. It was a case of mistaken identity that would have cost us our sweet boy had the Lord not used Thomas that way. "Please, my dear, don't let him out of your sight. You are being watched," Thomas again warned.

Chapter 14

Who Are You People?

*"Be strong and courageous. Do not be afraid or terrified because of them, for the L*ORD *your God goes with you; he will never leave you nor forsake you."*

-Deuteronomy 31:6

I remember this day as an ordinary day that found me cleaning my house and praying as I did it. I was abnormally filled with peace and joy. It seemed I talked to the Lord the whole day as I was cleaning, and, of course, the top of my list was always the process for Jo. I had been cleaning for a few hours, when my cell phone began to ring and ring and ring. I had gotten used to a couple of rings and the phone stopping. It was the Ugandan way to call someone, let it ring for a couple of times, and hang up hoping you would return the call at your own expense. Each call cost money, and if we called them back, it wouldn't cost them a dime.

My arms were filled with laundry when the phone reached four rings, and I knew it was important. I dropped the laundry and picked up the phone. This conversation followed:

"Hello..."

"Hello this is XXX from the US Embassy in Kampala. We have received a phone call from the U.S. State Department about you and your family. Who are you people?"

"Well, let me catch my breath!"

I think I might have stuttered. I could not believe what I was hearing. She was not a soft, warm voice, but the accent was definitely American. That alone was nice to hear. She asked as if she was inconvenienced to have to be calling.

"Why are you in Uganda?"

I told her who we were and why we were here. I told her how long we had been here and what organization we were representing.

She proceeded, "We have received a call from your mom and uncle concerning your safety. Is the story we have been told true?"

I told her it was all true. She asked me to relay the story of what happened, and then, informed me she would be calling the local police to verify if my story was true. She said "IF" she finds it to be true, then, she is going to tell the police they had better make sure you Americans are safe, not one hair on our head had better be touched. What we didn't know was right before this event with us, there had been a tragic event that had taken place in a part of the world called Benghazi. I'm sure this was in the forefront of their minds. She ended her conversation with me, stating, "The Embassy is not here to keep you safe. We aren't equipped for that. We are recommending you leave the country immediately due to your safety."

I told her we could not do that, and the reason being, we were about three months away from finalizing our adoption. She said, in a very, rough tone, "Leave the kid." I told her we would not do that. We were the only family he knew, and we would not leave without him.

She said, "Are you rejecting the recommendation of the U.S. government?"

Without fear or hesitation, I emphatically said, "Yes." She then told me we needed to get to a safe house or hire military armed guards. She advised, "If you can get to a safe house, don't tell anyone where you are. And when all your paperwork is together, make it to the airport at night and tell NO ONE! We've had people pulled off planes before. You aren't safe until the wheels of your plane are off the ground."

I sat there with my mouth on the floor. I could not believe what I was hearing. Her words were playing over and over in my head. "The embassy is not here to keep you safe." "Get to a safe house." "Not safe until the wheels are off the ground." All of this was a shock to me. All the movies I had seen in my lifetime where Americans ran to the embassy for safety were all fantasy...or at least, for Uganda. I had lived my life believing Americans were a different breed. We lived and died for our countrymen, but in that moment, I felt alone and shamed by my own country, for being in Uganda. It was a shock to my system and if I stayed in this moment of darkness, I would have been crushed.

Her words once again pierced my soul and anger began to surge through me like lightning, "Leave the kid." Wait, what? OH. NO. SHE. DIDN'T!!!! just tell me to leave my child and flee to safety. Satan would just love it if we just turned tail and ran. No way! This family would stand shoulder to shoulder and face the waves. We would do it without fear and we would win. We knew the Lord had called us to the journey, and we would leave when He told us to leave and not a day sooner.

Chapter 15

It's a Boy!

"I prayed for this child, and the Lord has granted what I asked of him."

-1 Samuel 1:27

April 23, 2013: Court Day

Could this actually be the day?

We have been here before, but this time, it felt different. I can't explain it, but I felt like this would be the day we would get further than we had ever gotten before. The day was bathed in prayer from people around the world and we knew God had the conclusion before the day had even started. We had to be there at 9am with Joseph's grandmother. If we could have the parents there as well, it would just be icing on the cake, but to find them and communicate with them would be a miracle. As it turns out, God had that very miracle waiting for us as we got out of our car.

Rehema was with us and smiled at Joseph the whole way there. She was a doting grandmother, if only from a distance. Her joy was overwhelming and the language barrier between grandmother and grandson would not stop her from trying to engage with him. It was so precious to watch her love for him. It filled up every crevice of that car. I did everything I could to make sure that this moment was burned into my memory. This is a moment I will tell Joseph about when he is older.

We pulled into the parking lot and parked towards the back of the building. We all piled out of the car and started to walk to the courthouse. Before I knew it, Rehema's smile melted into absolute terror. She began to point and speak in Luganda, with emotion that needed no translation. I had no idea what she was saying, but I turned to see what had caused such an emotional reaction. The person I saw coming towards us was the birth father, Mickdard. I kept telling her in English it was going to be okay, but she could not understand a word I was saying. Her emotional reaction was so great, I thought she would pass out. Before I knew it, Mickdard was before us, and she was on her knees before him.

I shouldn't have been shocked, but the sight in front of me was overwhelming. This sweet woman was in complete terror from this man, yet, was forced to give him the traditional Ugandan greeting when a woman meets a man on the road whom she knows. My American instinct kicked in when I saw her on her knees before him. I reached down and said, "Oh no, not today. Get up, get up!" I couldn't handle seeing the sight of this precious woman being forced to be submissive to a man who had obviously caused her so much pain.

With all my might, I tried to get her off the ground, however, she stayed like the perfect Ugandan woman does until the man acknowledges her. She slowly got up and tried very hard to tell me who he was, but unbeknownst to her, we had already met. I don't know the depths of their history. I know the obvious, but I don't know what else was behind this terrifying reaction. I wonder if she thought he had come to take Joseph back. Yet, we knew he was there to approve our adoption.

As we continued to walk into the courthouse, another surprise stood before us. It was Joseph's birth mother, Aisha. There it was, the miracle we had all prayed for. All the players were there, or so we thought.

When we finally made it into the building, we found our attorney was nowhere to be found. Unfortunately, he was on a bus coming from Kampala, and it was late. We ended up keeping the Judge waiting for an extra thirty minutes. She was far from happy about the tardiness. When our attorney finally did make it into the judge's chambers, he was a sweating, shaking mess. This poor guy was so nervous as he fumbled through his case for our file. I felt bad for him.

The room was hot and filled with family. The family that Joseph was born into this life with, that could no longer care for him, and the new family, who would love and walk him through the rest of it. Against the wall sat Joseph's birth parents, along with a new baby the mother recently had with a new man she was seeing. Rehema sat next to us. Emily and Morgan were also with us to witness this beautiful moment.

The judge had already read the file and became familiar with the extreme conditions Joseph had been through. However, the judge had our attorney read line by line Joseph's history anyways. She requested the police file photo from when he was rescued. The picture is so difficult for anyone to look at, including a seasoned, family court judge, and she nearly had a heart attack. She became so angry with the birth parents, telling them they need to be arrested and spend a significant time in prison. She sat there a few minutes before she expressed, she would have to think about this case and would see us back in her chambers on Monday morning. We all walked out in silence and knew Monday could mean any day she was ready to give us the verdict.

The wind was totally out of my sails. Waiting should have become second nature, but I always hoped for more in this whole process. Our attorney said that she had already made up her mind but was upset he was late. She was going to make us wait like we made her wait. I'm now wondering if there was more to it than that, but it did not negate the fact we were still waiting for the verdict.

Monday came, and we were at the courthouse ready and waiting. To our surprise, our judge was there and ready to give us the news we had waited two years to hear. She read her ruling, looking up at us and said, "My ruling is for you. It is clear that you have a family bond with this child, and you are the best for him." Tears began to stream down my face as I grabbed baby Joseph and hugged him like a crazy person. My son! According to the high courts of Uganda, he was now our son! Brian looked up at her and said, "Thank you so much. Can I give you a hug?" Before she could answer he was behind her desk with his arms wrapped around her. I think it's safe to say, we will be the family she never forgets.

We headed back to our house where I felt like I was coming home from the hospital with my newborn. I couldn't wait to tell the world God had answered all the prayers ever prayed for this sweet child. I got online and began my post, "IT'S A BOY..."

Chapter 16

Bad News: Disappearing Passport

Good News: That Bathroom Has AC

"For his anger lasts only a moment, but his favor lasts a lifetime; weeping may stay for the night, but rejoicing comes in the morning."

-Psalm 30:5

Since we had been named legal guardians of Joseph, we could now apply for his Ugandan passport. I wish with all my heart you could see the immigration office. Just thinking back to this place makes me break out in a sweat. It was controlled chaos at best. I remember being shuffled from office to office to get this done. We had a million forms to fill out, wondering just how passports are actually made in this country. We found people to help us, thinking it would make the process go faster, but in the end, it took a total of seven weeks to get the passport in our hands. As it turns out, while we were there, the Ugandan Feds were too. The passport division was closed down for weeks after we submitted our paperwork. It was closed down for corruption of all things.

Corruption runs deep in that country. Why now do they decide to do something about it? The frustration hits an all time high, and I think I might lose my mind. We get word that our paperwork is lost in the debacle and will have to start over. In order to receive a passport in Uganda, you have to have the Local Chief from the village you are in, write a letter of recommendation for you. We have to track him down again, pay him for his trouble, and head back up to Kampala.

We get there and again, are shuffled from office to office. No one can help us, and we have to submit another application. We waited another seven weeks until we got word from a man on the inside of the immigration office, that there was a passport waiting for Joseph. I was not going to believe it until it was in my hand. Once again, Brian and I made the three-hour trip to the capital city. We waited in a sea of people as the employees dug through piles of passports until they found his.

Their filling system was literally, piling up hundreds of passports on a wooden table, and opening them one by one until they found the name they were looking for. The sight of them digging for such a valuable treasure caused me to hold my breath. I held it until they held up their hand with pride indicating they had completed their daunting task. When they handed it to us, it was like we had won the lottery. The winning ticket was given to us, and I would guard it with my life. We knew the instant it was put into our hands we could apply for his American Visa. Now, that process was not going to be an easy one either, but I was more prepared for that than any other thing we had done so far.

The American Embassy was like stepping into a piece of America. I loved it, even though, it was scary and unsure. The one thing you can count on is Americans don't work in offices without AC. That's right, every office has central air. It was amazing, but what was even more wonderful, was the bathroom. It was your standard, American, public bathroom. Okay, maybe not standard, but this one was CLEAN and had AC. It had stall walls that weren't covered in the previous person's bathroom experience. I could not believe I had even missed American public restrooms. What is wrong with me?

Anyways, we were warned by fellow Americans of just how this process worked. We would be called into a tiny room where you stood in front of bulletproof glass, slid our file and application through what looked like an old bank window, and answer questions through a vented hole, as the woman thumbed through our file. She thumbed through it, and why I thought we were home free, I will never know. She pulled two forms out and told us they would have to be redone due to the fact they were in Lugandan. It meant we left without achieving our goal...once again. We had to go find our attorney, get him to rewrite the paperwork in English, pay him nearly $200 more to do it, and make another appointment with the U.S. Embassy, to start again. With weary, tired hearts, we scooped up our paperwork and made our way to the attorney's office.

We had just come through a seven-week delay and knew we were facing another period of an undetermined amount of time before we were going to be able to return to the U.S. Embassy. We were so discouraged. We wanted it now. We wanted the waiting to end and this journey to be over. Just one of the things we learned along the way was, we might be ready, but we weren't the only ones in this story. We began to understand, God was working in the lives of others, not just us. We had to trust the process, as I heard God say so many times before. We knew, as He was working in us and for us, He was getting everything else ready for our return to the U.S.

I can't remember how long it took for us to get the paperwork back from the attorney, but it was no less than three weeks. When the paperwork was given to us, we made that appointment with the Embassy and once again, stood in front of that bulletproof glass. As we stood there, this time, we had the translated paperwork, his medical clearance needed to travel, and two extra people in the waiting room in case they were called in for questioning.

Chapter 17

V-I-C-T-O-R-Y VISA

"For the LORD your God is the one who goes with you to fight for you against your enemies to give you victory."

-Deuteronomy 20:4

The day started early, and we knew anything could happen. This was the first time we were making the trip with a van full of people. We were told from everyone who came before us, we needed to have the birth family at the embassy in case the authorities needed them for questioning. The Embassy wanted to make sure we didn't pay them for their permission to adopt Joseph or offer them any type of bribe. The birth parents had to be in the waiting room with us. If we seemed suspicious in any way, it would be another delay.

So, we loaded up the van on that bright and sunny day with Rehema, Mickdard, Edward, who was our Kenyan friend and translator, and his friend who had come from the U.S. to visit him. We weren't sure how that would go since Rehema's reaction to Mickdard was so dramatic the first time she saw him. To our surprise, it was a very cordial greeting. The only thing this Jjaja (the African spelling for grandmother) cared about, was her little grandson, with whom she would get to spend the day. Squeals and excited giggles are universal. The way she would say his name to get his attention, led you to know exactly how she felt about him.

Mickdard on the other hand, sat talking to Edward our translator. Mickdard seemed to be a quiet and calm man, but we were sure he felt overwhelmed and unsure of the situation he was now in. He made little effort to interact with his birth son who was sitting in the seat behind him. I did notice, however, during the long, three-hour car ride he tried to sneak a couple of glances towards Joseph. I can only imagine the thoughts that must have been going through his mind as we made this long journey.

We made our way into the bustling city with cars and people in every direction. The sounds and smells of Kampala were very overwhelming. Edward and his friend had things to get done so, we dropped them off and made arrangements to meet back up for lunch when our appointment was done. Before Edward got out of the car, he explained to Mickdard and Rehema what was going to take place. They nodded and smiled at Edward, as he closed the door, and headed in the direction he needed to go.

As we made our way down Embassy Road, I felt the butterflies go wild. I knew what it took to get all of these people here today, and, if they turned us down, I wasn't sure we could get them all back for another try. I sat in silence and pleaded with God to allow this to be the day that made all of our blood, sweat, and tears -- a lot of tears -- worth it. We all got out of the van, making our way to the front gate of the U.S. Embassy. The American flag was flying high and proud. We had to show the armed guards our passports and our appointment sheet. We also had to explain who the Ugandans were with us and why they needed to be let in. It was just the first of many checkpoints we would have to pass through.

We all proceeded through the metal detectors and walked out of the glass doors which led us into a beautiful little park setting. We followed the path around until it led us to the same building we were in last time, the time we walked out in defeat. I had no idea how it would turn out this time, but we completely trusted God and His timing. This was a different emotion than last, complete trust no matter what! We walked in, turned in our appointment sheet, and took a seat. We watched how, one by one, different parties went into the little, glassed in rooms with arms full of children and paperwork. As I sit here and write this, I can feel the nerves I felt all those years ago.

Then, without warning, our names were called. Brian grabbed Joseph; I grabbed the paperwork. We walked into the little room and again, found ourselves facing the bulletproof window. Brian sat Joseph down on the ledge used for signing documents, and we were asked to raise our right hand as we were sworn in. We then, slid the giant packet of documents through the window slot and watched nervously as an American woman went through each document.

The woman behind the glass happened to be the very woman months earlier who, had called us and told us to get out of the country because we weren't safe anymore. I knew who she was, but I wondered if she remembered our names. That, we will never know. As she flipped through about twenty pages, we painstakingly put together, Joseph sat happy and calm just talking about everything he could think of. His sweet, little, four-year-old voice filled the little cubicle as I was a nervous wreck.

I looked at Brian and whispered to him to make him be quiet. Brian looked at me sternly and whispered back, "NO!" I wondered why Brian reacted that way until, the lady had finished our packet and looked up at us in absolute surprise. She said, "I have never heard a Ugandan child speak with an American accent before." Brian told her it's because Joseph had been with us before he could speak. She thought it was the most amazing thing. Brian then turned to me, and with gritted teeth whispered, "That's why I wanted him talking. She needed to hear his accent. You can't put him back in the village sounding like that."

She then said to us, "Is the biological family here today?" We told her, "Yes." Her reply, "THEY ARE?" We repeated our answer. She was so surprised. Yes, we covered our entire basis and would leave with nothing but victory today, so we hoped. She then asked to speak to Joseph in which I became really nervous. Would he talk to her? He didn't like to talk to people he didn't know. (He's still that way.) We slid him over to the hole in the window and the embassy lady began her questioning.

"Joseph, do you want to go to America?"

"Yes!" Joseph happily replied.

"If I let you go, will you be a good boy and not kick the chair in front of you the whole plane ride there?"

"Yes, I will be good, and no, I won't kick the chair."

"Then Joseph, I will give you permission to go to the United States," she said. I just about screamed my face off! The moment we had crossed another hurdle had come. She then told us the visa would be ready in a week and we could pick it up then. She also informed us she was going to give us a packet when we returned next week, that would have an official seal on it and it could only be broken by the custom's officer at our point of entry back into the United States.

She informed us the Ugandan customs officers at the airport will try to open it so we were to prepare another packet just for them. She also said these customs officers had been giving families a hard time and threatening to not allow them to leave. She quickly scribbled down a phone number and passed it through the window. She told us, "This is the embassy number. If they keep you from leaving, call us right away. Good luck in America. Joseph, make me proud." Joseph had no idea what she was saying, but nodded that chubby little face of his and said, "OK!"

We walked out of that dark room with victory and smiles that lit up the whole place. I very happily looked at Rehema and told her we received what we needed. I knew she didn't know what I was saying, but joy is universal and needs no translation. A week later, we returned, and just like the U.S. Embassy woman said, the packet was officially sealed, and the bright, beautiful American Visa for Joseph was stamped and ready to go. I wanted to jump through the window, but this time, it was to hug her and thank her for giving us the keys we needed to head back home.

I will never forget that walk back to the car. This time, it was filled with overwhelming joy and tears of thankfulness, not frustration. We sat in the hot car for a minute to take it in, and I turned and looked at Brian and said, "We stood before two governments and asked for their permission to adopt Joseph. They both said yes, when people told us it would never be done." The verse God had given me two years ago, while sitting in the immigration office, facing deportation, due to a work permit issue, came flooding back. "You will face heads of governments. They will fight you, but they will not win." It was a battle we fought every day since the day we said we would adopt Joseph, but it was worth it! We drove home with what I considered to be the golden ticket and knew we would now have to figure out how we would get plane tickets home. But first, to announce to the world, the Visa was ours, and we would soon be homeward bound.

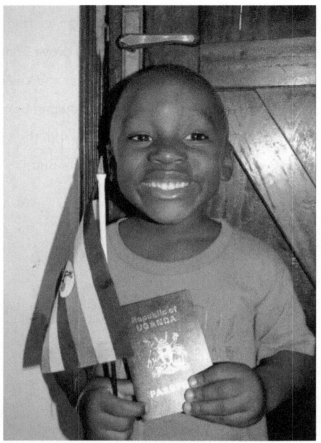

Joseph finally got his passport! V-I-C-T-O-R-Y VISA!

Chapter 18

Tickets Home

"And my God will meet all your needs according to the riches of his glory in Christ Jesus."

-Philippians 4:19

"That is why, for Christ's sake, I delight in weaknesses, in insults, in hardships, in persecutions, in difficulties. For when I am weak, then I am strong."

-2 Corinthians 12:10

For the first time since we had been in Uganda, the car ride home felt different. We were riding on an emotional high, a feeling we were not used to anymore. If it weren't for the potholes in the road, I would have thought we floated all the way home. During our three-hour trip home, I had gone over and over in my head how I would announce to the world that the Visa was ours. We had some of the best prayer support during our time there and I couldn't wait to tell everyone who was on pins and needles with us.

Upon arriving home, I didn't know if we would come home to electricity or not, but, also for the first time, I didn't care. I was not going to let anything steal the joy and victory of this moment. I eventually made it to the computer and announced on Facebook, our prayers had been answered. The Visa was in our hand and as soon as we were able to buy tickets, we would be heading home.

We were never good at raising money. In fact, that is the one thing we hated most of all about being missionaries. We knew, however, if we were going to make it home, it was going to take a village. We arrived in Uganda on a one-way ticket, which I know was God's plan, so I wouldn't jump ship on those darkest days (both physically and emotionally). For our family, there was no way in or out until God opened the door. He had put us there, and He would lead us home when He was ready. We once again asked the world to pray for us as we needed to purchase tickets to get home. Our work had come to an end and the adoption was ours. The only thing left was to get home.

It was only a matter of a couple of hours when we received word that enough money was given to buy our first ticket home. Letters of prayer and support came rolling in. We could not believe the overwhelming love and support we were shown. We can't thank people enough for walking with us during this journey. We still thank God for all of you and the way you stayed with us in the trenches.

In two days, we had all the money raised with five tickets purchased. I think I sat at the computer with my chin on my chest for way too long. God did it! When the timing is His, everything just comes together. I knew only He could open that door and do it instantaneously. We were scheduled to leave Uganda during the first week of July. We had two months to get things ready.

Chapter 19

The Safe House

"But let all who take refuge in you be glad; let them ever sing for joy. Spread your protection over them, that those who love your name may rejoice in you."

-Psalm 5:11

The words of the U.S. Embassy were always playing in the background of our minds, "Get to a safe house as fast as you can." The attempts people had gone through to take our lives had, in turn, taken a greater toll on us than we realized. When we knew the tickets were purchased and we emptied our house through selling or giving away our items, we were ready to go into seclusion until the day of departure. We came into the country with twelve, giant sized duffle bags, and we would leave with that plus one. I couldn't believe it. Here I was again giving away everything we had owned in Uganda. Just two years before, we had done the same when we left California. We had no idea we would do it all over again so soon.

We really thought our adventures in Uganda would last so much longer than it actually did. Watching our belongings walk out the door this time didn't have a tearing away effect like it did in America. I grieved the loss of my American, material possessions. The precious things we built our house with along with our nineteen years of marriage left in the hands of family and strangers. With each item, I had to say my goodbyes and trust I had just given them to God. I'm so sentimental that it nearly broke my heart in half. I know it must sound like an episode of "Hoarders", but I assure you it was not that.

It was the fact that I remembered God's faithfulness in every piece of furniture. It was the chairs I rocked my babies in. It was the table we ate at as a family and played games together (which later scared my kids from "Family Game Night"). We prayed, dreamed, and cried around that table. It was the red couches that God had given to us when I trusted Him for more than hand-me-downs. This process showed me that my life in America was built around belongings, and I didn't like that about myself. By the time we left for Uganda, there was no longer a hold on me where my stuff was concerned. I felt free and was ready to walk into the unknown with God and my family.

This time around, on the other side of the world, I gladly watched our home dwindle until there was nothing left but our echoes. The joy didn't come from the fact we were heading back to the USA, it came from the fact our things didn't hold me hostage. They were going to people who so desperately needed and wanted them. I was so excited to watch the faces of Ugandans and Westerners alike, leave with hard to find things. I knew and understood their emotions. Through the emptying of two houses in two years, it revealed to me that I had grown and was bound to nothing this world had to offer. I was free in a way I had never known or realized I needed.

During our time of emptying our Uganda house, we had fellow missionary friends that had a beautiful house just sitting there, empty of people, yet, fully furnished. This family had gone home to the Netherlands on leave. We had kept in touch with them, and they were aware of our situation. One day the phone rang, and it was our friends asking if we wanted to use their house as our hidden safe house, since they weren't there and would not be returning for months. It was going to be like being on vacation.

They lived on the road that nearly never ran out of power. The property was beautiful. It looked like we were at a resort. The house was painted and decorated like something you would not normally see in Uganda. But what really captured me was the peace that filled every room of the house. Peace was something we needed so badly as we re-entered the world, we had left a few years before.

We loaded up our van with our thirteen duffle bags, a few kitchen supplies, and our three kids. We took in the sights of the compound that had been our home for two years. It was beautiful. It sat on a hill that had a constant breeze. Next to the Lord, we think this breeze is what kept the mosquitoes away and the reason we never contracted malaria. Or was it the bats that lived in our attic?

Our gated compound came with two guest houses and two bunnies in the front yard. I had to move to Uganda to have a house with a guest house. I then realized, if we ever build our own house, it will have a guest house. How did I ever live without one?

As I took one final deep breath of the smoky, breezy air of Katwe, I was filled with so many amazing memories we made there. And just like that, we drove out of our gate one final time. The drive to the "safe house" was only a couple of minutes, but it felt like we had left home again into the unknown. We were starting the final ten days of our time in Uganda and knew we had to make the most of it. And we would be doing it with unlimited electricity!

Chapter 20

Our Final Days

"But Ruth replied, "Don't urge me to leave you or to turn back from you. Where you go I will go, and where you stay I will stay. Your people will be my people and your God my God."

-Ruth 1:16

Normally, the final days of where you have been, are packed with getting in the "lasts" of all your favorites. The restaurants you love, the final souvenirs, the glimpse of an African sunset, the final bowl of my favorite banana dish, and so on. What if you are not leaving from vacation, but from the battlefield?

As I sit here and try to explain what our final ten days were like, I'm flooded with every emotion I felt in those moments. It was rest, but on guard. We were so exhausted and battle weary. We knew at any moment anything could go south so we waited with guarded anticipation. It was full of joyful sounds, yet muffled sounds. It was full of thinking and planning for the days ahead, but not dreaming with hope. It was planning on shaky ground. The not knowing was the worst in every situation of our journey. We were excited to see our loved ones but, could we truly go home again? I thought about some of our final moments we spent saying goodbye for what might be the last, last time. So, the final days were not spa days. They were full of God's grace and sufficiency for us.

We knew one of our goodbyes was going to lead us back into the Muslim village Joseph was born in. I had to get back there and hug Rehema one more time. I had to thank her for trusting me with her most precious gift. Her grandson. I had to let her know I would always love her as my family too. I had to promise that I would never take her gift for granted. I knew it was a gift of great price. It was a gift that broke years of tradition and bondage. It was a gift leading to freedom. It was a gift with divine purpose and Kingdom rewards. She had to know I fully understood the value of her sacrifice.

We loaded up our van with our kids, Edward our amazing friend and translator, and every gift I could think that would bless her life. We brought her fabric and buttons for a new dress. We purchased bags of sugar which was like gold to them. We brought her tea and a very ornate teacup (absolutely not practical, but it was so beautiful, and I wanted her to have something beautiful). I wanted her to think of us every time she used it, but I bet it's still in the box it came in, sitting in her very, primitive showcase cabinet. And we also brought two, head scarves with sparkles, of course.

As we pulled up, we could hear her screams of joy coming from inside the house. In a nanosecond, she was at the car, waiting for hugs from us. Right away, I noticed this visit was going to be different from the first one. Where were all the towns' people? We were greeted this time with just a few family members. It didn't bother me, but it was a stark contrast to the very first visit over a year earlier. This time there was an atmosphere of peace and joy. She quickly took us in and sat us down.

I was like a proud little girl bringing her mother a basket of gifts I couldn't wait for her to open. But to my surprise, she was not yet interested in the gift. Though they were presented to her, and Edward explained the basket; it wasn't the basket that had captivated her attention. It was the sweet chubby bouncing four-year-old boy, dressed in overalls that she cared about. The love and care that poured out of this grandmother's smile was unmistakable. You knew her every thought when she looked at Joseph. This woman looked at him with a love and devotion I had never seen. Not even from new moms holding their first baby.

I don't know their history before I got to Uganda, but I know Joseph was born in that house and she must have helped with the delivery. I know this was her first grandchild and it was a boy, on top of that. By the look on her face, I knew there was a story, but I may never fully know just what these two went through together, before JoJo was forced to leave the village. She finally made it back around to the gift basket and was very grateful for all the gifts. But nothing was going to top the gift in the room that had a bald head, toothy grin, and dressed in overalls.

To our surprise we weren't going to spend the day at that house. She had planned a day for us across the village at the house of the woman she called, "Mom". Sometime during the day, she explained to me that the woman was really her mother's sister. Her mother had died years before, and her aunt stepped in and became her mother. We pulled up to a house that was so much more grand than the house Joseph was born in. We were welcomed by a few kids and a round jolly woman who had eyes that would sparkle when she smiled. I thought right away that I loved her personality, and we hadn't said one word to each other that we understood. The woman turned out to be Rehema's cousin and they loved being together, just like sisters.

The women took us right away and showed us the little farm they lived on. To our surprise we noticed a good-sized pig pin and about eight pigs. I looked at Brian and said, "Look at the pigs! This side of the family is not

Muslim!" Our tour continued around the beautiful homestead. It came with running, laughter, and tons of smiles. The kids and family members who had never imagined a day with Joseph seemed to be in a state of unspeakable joy. Before we were brought into the house for lunch, we stopped to take pictures with grandmas, aunties, and cousins.

We were taken into a fairly, large sitting room where we had sweet conversation with Joseph's grandmother and great aunt, thanks to Edward. Rehema walked away for a few minutes and returned with a bowl of water, sitting down in front of Joseph, where she gently took his little hands and began to wash them. It was such a sweet moment to watch. She was beaming from ear to ear as she did it. She took her time as if she didn't want the moment to end. She was such a sweet, loving, and doting grandmother. She was getting her little first-born grandson ready for lunch.

In the next moment, she had presented him with the first plate of food for this meal. She wished with all her heart Joseph could talk back to her, but her love and actions spoke louder than any other words could have. We were all presented with food they had so lovingly and painstakingly made for us, on a charcoal stove (more like a pot), at the back of the house. As they cooked, I could hear the joyful banter between them, and I wanted so badly to know what their sweet giggles and words were all about. We sat on the floor and ate our lunch knowing this was another first we were taking part in.

After lunch, they wanted to take us on a walk which led us through a part of the village I had never seen. As we walked down the bright, red, clay road, people from the village came out of their homes and stood with surprised looks on their faces. One villager spoke to Rehema and she answered back with a proud voice and a sweet chuckle in her voice. Edward said the village woman wanted to know where she got those Mzungus (Mzungus, meaning, "Where you got those "white people?"")? Rehema's reply was, "These are MY mzungus!"

We continued to walk through the village until we ended up at a beautiful garden of passion fruits. That's when Edward told us they were farmers and sold their produce in the marketplace for income. Passion fruit is not only the best fruit I have ever had but is also grown in the most beautiful way. Passion fruit requires growing on a trellis, which is, a framework of wood or metal bars, mainly used to support fruit trees or climbing plants. At full bloom, you end up with a beautiful canopy type tunnel garden, full of this hanging fruit. It grows on all sides and overhead. It makes for the most beautiful pictures.

As soon as we arrived there, the two sister cousins ran through this beautiful canopy garden, picking the fruit as fast as they could. They first grabbed a giant banana leaf from a tree and rolled it into a makeshift basket, filling this cone shaped leaf with as many fruits as it would hold. When they had filled these leaf cones, they began using the extra pieces of fabric on their dresses to hold their fruit bounty. As they picked, these women danced, teased, and laughed with each other. I tried to take as many pictures in the moment as I could. These women danced

168

as if they were ten-year-old girls without a care in the world. They danced in a sense of freedom that was absolutely breathtaking. This was a moment in time I didn't want to come to an end, but unfortunately, we had to head home before dark.

Sadly, our day was coming to an end. Rehema was not going to let the doting over Joseph stop, so she helped him into the van and spotted a sand bucket full of Hot Wheel cars. I told her the little cars were his absolute favorite toys. She lit up with excitement and cupped her hands to her mouth with shock, explaining to us Joseph's aunt was a Rally car, race driver. In fact, the house we were visiting with the passion fruit vineyard happened to be owned by her, but she currently lived in Kampala.

There it was, so many mysteries solved in one statement. The house was grand because it was bought with her winnings. Joseph's love for cars and his love for fast sports cars must have been genetic. The memory that instantly popped into my mind was of the first day we had him at our house. We needed toys for him so Morgan let him play with his Hot Wheel cars. We weren't sure if Joseph was going to know what to do with them, but then he scooted himself off the couch, turned around, and began to make car noises, rolling a car back and forth.

We all looked at each other in shock. We weren't aware of any toy cars at the baby home, but he instantly knew how to play with it. It was in his blood all along. To this day, Joseph's love for cars is still strong. In fact, his taste for fast, high dollar cars is in full gear. He's praying we buy him a Bugatti Veyron. It's safe to say that a three-million-dollar car won't be coming from us, but a boy can dream!

We pulled out of the driveway, and as we were driving down the road, Edward began to tell us of a conversation he had had with Rehema. She had told him she was not born into the Muslim faith but had married into it. She went on to tell him, now that we are in her life, we are now her family and because of us, she will be a Christian and stand behind us as family. What she continued to say took my breath away and still brings tears to my eyes.

She told him that when Joseph was born, she knew she would never be allowed to help raise him due to the fact her daughter was unwed. She knew Joseph would be banished from the village. Rehema then began to pray God would send someone to love and raise this sweet baby because she would never get that chance. She asked God to save her grandson, and two years' time, she was able to see God work in a way she never thought possible. Here, we thought we were chosen to help set him free, when all along, the first prayer for freedom started in a secret place in the heart of a grandmother who knew that if God did not answer her prayer, this sweet baby would die. So, out of an undying love, she sacrificed her birthright and told the Lord, "I can't raise him so please send someone who will."

Out of all the people in the world, we were chosen for this child. Who is he? Who will he become? His life was saved for purpose. I wondered, did Moses' mom cry out to

God with the same prayer as Rehema prayed? All of this washed over my heart as we made the trek back to Masaka. I knew this woman was forever my family, and I will do my best to honor her as we raise her boy!

On the right: Joseph's grandmother, Rehema. On the left, Rehema's aunt who stepped in and raised Rehema. She calls her mom. In the middle, Rehema's cousin. All cheeks.

Rhema and her Aunt/Mom, standing in the orchard of hanging passion fruit, hanging from wooden trellis.

Rehema and her cousin holding passion fruit. They are picking all of this fruit to give to Joseph. It was a gift. Just a way they showed their love. We left with a minivan full of passion fruit.

Rehema, standing in the orchard of passion fruit.

Rehema, washing Joseph's hands.

Jokingly called "His family roots." This tree was dubbed, "Joseph's Tree" by Rehema. JoJo loved playing and standing on the roots of this tree, located by his birth home.

Chapter 21

Father to Father

"And over all these virtues put on love, which binds them all together in perfect unity."

-Colossians 3:14

We had only two days left in Uganda, and the day started with a phone call for Edward telling us that the birth father is requesting a meeting with us. We were so nervous with that call because at any moment, he could change his mind, no matter what papers were signed, and we could lose Joseph.

We set the meeting for 2:00pm at the pool sight of our Danish friends. Behind this giant gate sat the most beautiful pool with little huts/cottages that could be rented to visitors. It held many memories of parties and the days we just needed to escape. It would be neutral ground, and we asked Edward and the Baby Home owner

179

to be there with us in case we needed it. Mickdard is his name and he is a quiet man. But behind those eyes, he is a thinker. He longs for more but has never gone after anything that wasn't instant gratification.

He was the first to speak. He spoke in clear English, without the aid of Edward. Talk about surprised. He could speak English this whole time. He understood everything we were saying all along. I hate that he hid that due to not feeling confident. We could have had so many more conversations.

The surprises were not over. Out of his pocket, he pulled out a stack of papers. In Uganda, a way to show you are making better life choices is to buy land. He brought the papers with him as proof he was changing his life. He said, "I don't understand how you can treat me with love when I tried to kill this boy. I don't understand how you can love a child that is not your own, but you do. Because of the love you have shown me, I want to be a different man. I know you are leaving for America, and I had to tell you before you left, that I am changed because of you. I even bought land. I need to prove that I'm changing my ways. I had to bring you here today to show you the deed and to tell you I'm sorry for hurting this child. Even though, I never laid a hand on him, I knew that his step-mother was trying to kill him while I looked the other way. I don't want you to leave Uganda without me getting to tell you that I'm so sorry for the pain I allowed this child to go through. I needed you to leave with a better memory of me, and you have to know I don't understand your love, but I am changed because of it."

WHAT JUST HAPPENED?

I looked at Brian, with my chin on the table. Again, history was being made in front of our eyes and freedom was awakening. My eyes darted from Mickdard to Brian and back again. I was watching two fathers face each other with one common thread, a little boy who was not loved by one, but so deeply loved by the other. I was watching a father hand off the child to another father who would guard this child with his life. Who would love him as if he was bone of his bone and flesh of his flesh. Mickdard gave him happily to Brian but didn't know why. Then Brian, my gentle warrior spoke, "I love you because my Bible says too. It tells me that God loved me first, so I am to love others. I believe the Bible is truth, and I live by its direction. Now, let me ask you a question. Do you believe in the Koran?"

Mickdard replied, "Yes, I do."

Brian then said, "Doesn't the Koran tell you that when you first met me, you had to kill me because I wasn't a Muslim?"

"Yes, it does," he replied.

"Why didn't you then?" Brian asked.

"I don't know. I'm really confused and now must go back and read what the Koran says comparing with how I am able to sit here with you in peace and how I have been told that you are my enemy."

In my sheltered mind, I would have never thought a Muslim and a Christian would be sitting at the same table, let alone, speaking on the topic of love. Brian told him not to read the Koran, but the Bible, instead. That's where he would find the answers he was looking for. Brian then said to him, "Can I give you a hug?" The two fathers embraced, and I know all of heaven cheered at one time!

Our time with Mickdard had come to an end, but I found myself standing there, studying his face because this was the face of my new son's birth father. I didn't want to forget a thing. We took a picture together and said goodbye, one final time. Mickdard was not the only one changed that day. After that meeting, my heart was never the same. I was totally wrecked for the better.

Chapter 22

Perfect Love Casts Out All Fear

"There is no fear in love. But perfect love drives out fear, because fear has to do with punishment. The one who fears is not made perfect in love."

-1 John 4:18

As Edward dropped us off at our beautiful, hidden safe house he told me he had one more thing he must tell me before we headed home for America.

"Remember that day we went into the village for the first time? All the family was there and many villagers?" What he said next will forever be engraved into my heart and mind. He then continued, "They were all there to kill you."

I think it took a few minutes for those words to really penetrate my mind. I then replied with the biggest, "WHAT?" that I could let out with. "Yes," he said. "You had no idea the danger you all were in. All the family began talking at once, and I heard what they were saying. I knew the plans they had for you. All of them in the room looked at you and Brian and instantly, were filled with fear. They began yelling, 'Look at their eyes! Look at their eyes!'"

Edward couldn't see what they were seeing, but he instantly knew that the Holy Spirit showed up and cancelled the plans of the enemy. Edward said they continued yelling, "Why do these Mzungus look so different?" Brian and I could hear the volume in the room amp up, but we felt no fear. In my arrogance, I thought, "Wow, these people are so happy to see us!" Nope! Turns out, it was just the opposite.

I remember Edward talking back to them just as fast. "Those are the eyes of Jesus. You don't know Him, but you can't touch them." I could not believe all of this was happening right in front of us without us ever knowing. Edward then told me, "You and Brian were like little children playing in a pit of vipers. God hid the danger for you and you loved them with open arms. Then, you went back three more times and they threw you a party and prepared food for you."

Even as I write this, I'm still in shock of how God's hands were holding us as we walked through the "Valley of the Shadow of Death." He did prepare a table before us in the presence of people who wanted us dead, all the while, we feared no evil.

I think I stood there numb for a while. I allowed the memories of all the different trips into the village to flood my mind. It didn't matter how hard I tried, I couldn't remember there ever being a feeling of fear or being unwelcomed. I only felt joy and deep love for these people. God truly had shielded us so that we would love freely and without hesitation. Psalm 23 has a whole new meaning for me. I didn't know it would play out in such a tangible way.

We hugged Edward, our fearless Kenyan pastor (who, he himself escaped persecution and even, execution, by the hands of his countryman. Who fled to Uganda to become one of the greatest missionaries I have ever known), one last time and thanked him for all he had given to us during our time in Uganda. Without him, I don't know how the gap between the Muslim village of Nenzy and the Rowe family would have been bridged. God used him to stand shoulder to shoulder with us as we fought for one of the greatest gifts we have ever been entrusted with. No matter where life takes us, Edward will always be a part of our great story.

Chapter 23

The Final Goodbye

"I thank my God every time I remember you."

-Philippians 1:3

Two days later, our sweet friend showed up to take us and all thirteen bags to the airport. It was bittersweet leaving Masaka, one last time. We took the threat against our lives very seriously, and because of that, we couldn't say goodbye to all the Ugandan friends we had made along the way.

So, thank you beautiful, electronics lady we bought light bulbs from. You were the first Ugandan to not charge us the "skin tax," always treating us with love and respect.

Thank you, vegetable man, who went out of your way to find me my favorite produce and never cheat me because I was white.

Thank you, David, the electrician who got off a bus headed in the opposite direction, from Masaka, to come back and fix our power situation. Who faced an attic full of bats, so we could have restored power. You are my superhero!

Thank you, Peter Mukongo, who was our printer guy and friend. Because of you, we never ran out of ink as we printed a thousand forms. The list goes on and on.

We didn't think we would be leaving so soon, so we jumped into Masaka life as fast as we could and made friends with as many people as we could, upon arrival to Uganda. And we rolled out of town, as quiet and unnoticed as we rolled in, but in my heart, I thanked all the people who made this adventure a little easier for us.

Our friend Tyler took us to the airport to catch our 11pm flight to Brussels. He and his wife, along with our Danish friends were the only ones who knew we were leaving town. It was safer that way. We spent the time before the flight eating dinner and swimming at our favorite hotel. We had ice cream in Entebbe, one more time, and then, we pulled up to the airport door and unloaded my precious cargo and thirteen, body bag size, duffle bags. At this point, the words of the U.S. Embassy played over and over in my head, "If they try to keep you from leaving, call this number."

I knew, for several families, this is the point they were turned away. My blood pressure was off the charts and literally my hearing became muffled because of it. I knew we had one more hurdle to face. I shook as I filled out the custom forms and waited our turn to get our exit stamps placed in our passports. We had to present our adoption folder to the customs agent. All the paperwork had to be in exact order, or they would turn us away.

In the folder was permission from the Ugandan government and the U.S. government to leave Uganda with Joseph. I didn't want them to turn us away because they thought they could. So, I placed Jo's police file photo in front as shock value so the customs agent would understand that adopting him was absolutely necessary. When the lady opened the file she gasped and instantly became angry with me, like she knew what I had done. She said to me, with shock and anger in her voice, "This is not who he is any more. You no longer need to associate him with this picture any longer!" That's right I don't, but you need to know it was for his freedom. With great force she stamped all five passports and said, "Now leave!" The door was opened, and we were almost free.

We sat at the gate for over an hour. Once again, the words of the U.S. Embassy played in my mind, "You aren't safe until the wheels are off the ground. We have had people pulled off planes before." The time had come for us to board the plane. Joseph sat with me at the start of the flight. Emily and Morgan, who were never separated, sat giggling and picking out their in-flight movie. I looked for Brian who was directly behind Emily and Morgan.

The sight was comical. I still laugh as I write this. Brian was shoved into a two-seater with a terrified looking Muslim woman. Now that I mention it, Brian wasn't happy about it either. The flight was so empty it was as if we had the plane to ourselves. Due to seat vacancies, the sweet, little Muslim woman excused herself from that section of the plane and found her own seat.

The sweet flight attendant quickly walked past our seat. Joseph stopped her and very loudly said, "When do we eat?" With a very shocked look on her face, she said, "When we are in the air." After all I said to Joseph, that's what he held on to. We get to eat on the plane. Without a doubt, he was my boy.

Not long after settling in our seats, the Captain's voice was heard welcoming us aboard and telling us to fasten our seatbelts as take-off was at hand. The roar of the engines shook the plane where the force from the speed forced us all back in our seats. The look of thrill filled Joseph's four-year-old face. The moment we dreamed about was here. Liftoff was never sweeter. The wheels were off the ground, and I wanted nothing more than to high five Brian at that moment (but we weren't sitting together, and he doesn't do high fives!). I was sitting with my sweet Joseph Freedom. Wheels were up. Victory and freedom was ours!!!

Chapter 24

Welcome to America

"For I know the plans I have for you," declares the Lord, "plans to prosper you and not to harm you, plans to give you hope and a future."

-Jeremiah 29:11

We landed in Chicago. I could hardly believe it. My feet were on American soil once again. The first time Joseph felt America under his feet. We waited in the immigration line before handing our passports to a very, jolly man. We then handed our "official" file to him. He looked up at us again with joyful surprise and said, "Welcome home. Step over here."

We were then ushered to a different part of the airport that is not normally seen by the regular passengers. There, the official seal was broken in front of us and our paperwork was quickly gone through. I don't remember much after that. I feel a part of me checked out. We ran a race for two years. The finish line was handing over a file I guarded with my life, and when I had taken it as far as I could...I let go!

We boarded our last flight. We would be going home, not to California, but to Arkansas. The place I swore I would never return. The place I felt was my personal Egypt, but that is for another book.

As I sat on the plane, I talked to God and asked him why we were returning there? I know that was where all our family was, but why did we have to go back there? Could we ever truly go home again? So many emotions welled up inside of me. "Why God, why?" I didn't hear God right away, but He showed me a picture. I was dancing in a flower field with combat boots on wearing a sundress. Then I heard him, "This will be your hardest mission field yet."

The picture let me know we were still on the frontline, but we were going to find joy there too. My eyes filled up with tears and spilled down my cheeks. The next emotions were like nothing I had ever felt. I was home, but I felt the battle was still raging. What would I find there? The things that I would find there would be one of great joy, but also, great sorrow. As the wheels touched down at Clinton National Airport in Little Rock, Arkansas, I cried. I knew one of my greatest battles had come to an end, but I knew there was something coming that would cause me to lace up my boots like never before.

We exited the plane and walked towards a great cheering crowd. The crowd was filled with faces I had known my whole life and some I had only seen on Facebook. They weren't screaming my name, but the name of a baby they had prayed for, for two years. They prayed for freedom and standing before them was my little, Ugandan cherub of a boy, the fruit of their faith in flesh. With homemade "Welcome Home" poster board signs, declaring "Welcome to America." Finally, Joseph Freedom Rowe was home and FREE!

***

The people who got off that plane on the hot July day in 2013, in Arkansas, were not the same people who boarded the plane two years earlier. Those people were scared, arrogant American kids. We had no idea the freedom we would find by letting go of the world we came from and embracing the adventurous journey that lay ahead. Years ago, an artist by the name of Twila Paris sang a song called "The Warrior is a Child." That song described us to a "T".

God put us on the front line in armor that felt too heavy and ill fitting, but with each passing day, our faith grew, and our armor cinched up. Our fear began to disappear. We faced things we never thought we would have to confront. We stood with our backs straight as we faced two governments, and sought permission to adopt a child, who so desperately needed us as much as we needed him. We faced more warfare than we ever had in our entire life. At the end, we can say, we wouldn't trade it for the world. We are who we are because of it.

I would have never thought I could truly give up all my earthly possessions with joy to the Lord and move blindly to a country I had never been to before, that first day back in the summer of 2011. We learned to walk with the confidence of the Lord and in His security. We stopped listening to fear and fell into the deep end of faith. We stood in the African Savanna and saw animals only seen on the National Geographic Channel. We walked into a hostile village and walked out with family members.

From the beginning, this journey was so much bigger than we would have ever thought. We thought our dream of being missionaries was finally being fulfilled, and it was. But somewhere along the way, it turned into so much more than that. Everything we saw and did had one common thread. That thread was FREEDOM!

"It is for freedom that Christ set us free. Stand firm, then, and do not let yourselves be burdened again by the yoke of slavery."

-(Galatians 5:1)

-For Freedom-

Me (Angela) and Joseph. 2019. He was 10 years old.

Epilogue

(I know you are tempted to close the book and not read this section. After all, who reads the Epilogue? READ this Epilogue! You won't believe what happened.)

Eight years have come and gone since we first stepped foot in Uganda. I had always heard, once you return from Africa, you never really return. That "life" always seems to be with you. I have found this statement to be true. Yes, it was hard, but being on this side of it, I can truly say there are days I wish I could feel the red, clay dirt under my feet as I sit with a plate of my favorite cooked bananas.

The fall of 2019, we found ourselves in Fort Wayne, Indiana commissioned by the Lord to once again, begin a journey only He could author. The details of our next adventure might be saved for another book. I can assure you, it will not be boring as we are the Rowe family and boring is something we have not learned to do.

We had only arrived in Fort Wayne a few weeks, when I saw on Facebook, our beloved friend and translator Edward was flying into our new city. He was coming for a two month stay for farm training and some good old-fashioned relaxation. We surprised him the night he made it to his host family's house. We had not seen him for over six years. The joy and excitement was mutual when Edward, Brian, and I finally saw each other after all those years. But the breath-taking moment is when he laid eyes on Joseph again after six years.

Joseph left Uganda shortly after his fourth birthday and stood right below my waistline. The child Edward saw standing before him now was a ten-year-old boy with a deep voice who was nearly as tall as him. Edward gasped and yelled, "JOJO!" Joseph, who has never really been the touchy feely type of child, was then pulled into a hug legends are made of. Edward then went on to tell me it was like no time had passed. He thought Brian and I looked exactly the same as the day we left. That man knows how to stay close to my heart, and that is the ONLY lie I will tolerate.

We began to talk loud and fast as if our conversation had a time limit and as if we would spontaneously disappear from each other's lives once again. Once the shock Edward was going through had settled, he began to ask us why we had moved to Fort Wayne, and what we had been doing since he last saw us. We let him know of the things we had been doing and how returning home was just as much a growing time as living in Uganda. I let him know I had written a book about our time in Uganda about our adoption story. I used this time to let him know I had proudly and with much honor put him in our book.

He was so excited to hear this and then, began to say repeatedly, "I must get back to Joseph's village and tell the Jaja I have kept my promise. I HAVE KEPT MY PROMISE!!! I told her all those years ago you people were the best family for him and look at him now. I kept my promise!" Edward's joy was deep, and his word was his bond. He was going to let Rehema and the village know. I couldn't really grasp the eagerness in which he kept repeating himself.

We continued to reminisce about the first day we went into the village with him. He looked a little shocked as he had forgotten to tell me something and then, looked at me and said, "I must tell you...

"The day you went into the village and all the villagers were there to kill you (said so nonchalantly), I have to tell you what they saw." Edward then leaned up in his chair and pointed at me with such force, "YOU, every time you spoke, they were afraid. Remember how they began to yell, and the room got very loud?" I remember thinking at the time the whole room loved us and were so happy to see Brian and me. Yeah, well, that's not what he said next.

Edward began to speak again, "The village people were so afraid and said "Who are these people? Every time she talks to us, there is a man who stands in front of her smiling at us." Edward said he could not see what they were seeing, but he told them it was Jesus. Edward continued, "The grandfather was so afraid of you, he ran out of the house. I tell you, I heard this man on the phone making his plans to kill you both, and then Jesus came and stood in front of you. There was nothing else he could do but run. You came back to the village a few more times after that, and he told Rehema not to tell you he was there because he feared you."

I sat there with my mouth on the floor. I had to process this. Jesus came! What did He look like? They got to see Jesus!!! Edward said, "There is more you must know. Remember a few years ago you sent David and me back into the village with pictures of Joseph to give to the grandmother? That is when the village started to realize you not only cared for Joseph, but you loved them as well. You need to know, when Joseph received his citizenship, I was driving past the village and stopped to show the grandmother the picture. I let her know he was a U.S. citizen now.

She grabbed my phone and began yelling and running through the village. I had to chase her down to get my phone back. I asked her why she was acting this way. She let me know, for six years, the grandfather had been

205

beating her because she would not let him kill us. He became the butt of all the villagers' jokes. They called him loser because he would not stand up for Allah and kill the Christians. So, every time he was made to be the fool in town, he came home and beat her."

All the village came out to see Edward's phone where Rehema was able to tell them the news of Joseph. He had become an American. They all began to say, "WE REPENT! WE REPENT! We wanted the Americans dead, and you would not let us touch them. And because they lived, look at our boy. WE REPENT!" Edward then went on to tell us he has since cultivated a relationship with the grandfather. He was told the grandfather is still afraid of us and once word got to them about Joseph's life, he knew he must stop beating his wife because the Americans will return someday, and he will have to answer to us.

What just happened!!!!!!

Edward said the village now protects him, and if there is any trouble, this town will stand with him. I still shake my head as I write this. Love that these people do not understand, now makes them fight for Christians instead of against them. Everything these people ever believed is now in total question because it just doesn't line up anymore.

Edward is now the first Christian pastor ever to have full access to this village without the threat of death. He is their friend and one they will now die to protect. The village that once wanted us dead now calls us their family and looks forward to the day we come for a visit. Edward assures us they will throw us a huge reception out of love and respect. Whether the grandfather will be there is still to be determined.

Finding Freedom

About the Author

Angela lives in Fort Wayne, Indiana, with her husband Brian, of 28 yrs. They have 4 children. Two of them are married to wonderful spouses and they have just recently had their first grandchild. Angela and her family love spending time together in whatever capacity their schedules allow. In her spare time, she loves holding her grandbaby for hours on end, and without a doubt, she loves everything that sparkles.

Angela has always had a huge heart for people. She loves encouraging those around her to be fully what God has called them to be. She loves traveling to speak to various groups. At a young age, Angela felt the call to Missions. Her heart is not only for those around her, but also for the nations.

If you would like to contact Angela Rowe, please do so, by sending an email to: findingfreedom11@yahoo.com. Or, you may contact her through her Facebook, social media platform at:

www.facebook.com/angelacrowe.

Made in the USA
Las Vegas, NV
16 December 2021